D1607609

Fountain Publishers
P.O. Box 488
Kampala
E-mail:fountain@starcom.co.ug
Website:www.fountainpublishers.co.ug

Distributed in Europe, North America and Australia by African Books Collective Ltd (ABC), Unit 13, Kings Meadow, Ferry Hinksey Road, Oxford OX2 0DP, United Kingdom. Tel: 44(0) 1865-726686, Fax:44(0)1865-793298.E-mail:abc@africanbookscollective. comWebsite: www.africanbookscollective.com

ISBN 978-9970-02-720-0

Dictionary of Criminology

Mwene Mushanga

FOUNTAIN PUBLISHERS
Kampala

Introduction

In professional disciplines, just as in academics, the definition of basic concepts is fundamental for adequate understanding of issues. A dictionary of criminology may be regarded as irrelevant for the simple reason that criminology cannot be said to constitute an academic or professional discipline in East Africa. But this dictionary is not limited to criminological or sociological concepts alone. Just like any academic discipline, it covers other areas of social studies such as law, economics and politics. The dictionary covers some areas that, to the average reader, are least related to law and crime; but to the specialist, even the least likely entry, like race, tribe and democracy is, in some remote way, linked to the incidence of crime, delinquency or deviance. I am aware that eyebrows will be raised in some legal circles for inclusion of some of these entries, but I believe that an interdisciplinary approach to social issues is an inevitable development, for in the world we live in nothing is independent of other areas of human existence. The economic system affects politics, as it does health or education; the legal system is influenced by culture or education; and the religious aspects of the people concerned.

My interest in compiling this dictionary was to provide the student, the government official, those without legal training, the desk worker, or the professional legal consultant with a simplified text to which to refer for easy reference.

I must confess that I am thoroughly dissatisfied with the state of our knowledge, especially with the educated members of our society. We have a tendency to believe that if you are not a doctor of medicine you are not expected to know what a caesarian section or Hodgkin's lymphoma is; or that if you are not a lawyer you need not know what harbeas corpus is or the difference between rape and statutory rape. What we need to accept as time goes on, is that the monopoly of skills and technical know-how will remain the monopoly of the professionals, but the general public has the right to know what goes on in professional circles; for no one has a right to the monopoly of knowledge. It is said that a little knowledge is dangerous, but no knowledge at all is definitely more dangerous.

I have included some commonly used abbreviations that bothered me earlier in my academic life, words like e.g., viz, ibid., ergo, etc. The average reader comes across these brief words but may not readily know what they stand for. One could ask why some entries have brief definitions while others have longer descriptive definitions. This is because some words or concepts are considered to be less well understood, or because of their social, economic or legal importance need detailed definitions than others. For example, to explain how an individual gradually develops to become a criminal needs more explanation than the concept of abandon; the rule of law needs more explanation than arson. I have also included a few names of eminent scholars who have made enormous contributions to the study of crime, criminology, law and related disciplines, among whom are Lombroso, Garofalo, Sutherland, Sellin, Marx, Clinard, Wolfgang and others.

It is self-evident that without the contribution of such outstanding persons, criminology would not have grown to be the academic discipline and profession that it is today.

In compiling this dictionary, I have made use of a number of sources, textbooks of sociology, law, criminal justice, psychiatry and philosophy and, where appropriate, these sources have been indicated at the end of the relevant entry.

Mwene Mushanga
Kabwohe, 2007

Acknowledgement

My gratitude goes to my son Ndyabarema Mushanga, himself a lawyer, who did some editing, made comments on legal concepts and contributed some entries; and Miss Enid Kuribatura, secretary at Itendero Secondary School, who typed the manuscript; she had a hard time deciphering my hand writing, made worse by the fact that I only have 25 percent vision in both eyes.

Prof. Marshall B. Clinard, American elder brother, friend and teacher, himself an eminent scholar and distinguished professor of sociology and criminology at the University of Wisconsin, Madison, has been a source of inspiration and encouragement for the last forty years. His *Sociology of Deviant Behavior*, together with Robert F. Meier, which I first read as an undergraduate at Makerere, has been published for half a century and is now in its 11th edition; his *Crime in Developing Countries*, together with Daniel J. Abbott, based on research done in Uganda in the 1960s, is an excellent contribution to the study of crime in developing countries, and his *Corporate Crime*, together with Peter C. Yeager, is already a classic. Professor Clinard's contribution in the field of criminology ranks as high as that of Sutherland, Sellin, Mannheim and others. Professor Clinard wrote the introduction to my book *Criminal Homicide in Uganda* in 1974. I cherish our association.

Lastly, I want to thank my wife, Mama Muko, for her continued interest in my paperwork. I owe her a great deal.

Mwene Mushanga
Kabwohe, 2007

Preface

If I recall correctly, you were in charge of the adult education for north-west Uganda and I believe I said to you that you should be the first criminologist in Uganda and be a professor in the university. You and your family have always meant a lot to me and my family. I remember many incidents from our visits with you; we always had a great time together!

Your determination to achieve certain goals has been achieved in the face of many difficulties. You have had many tragedies in your family and you then took over many of the orphaned members, but you kept on with your work.

You opposed Amin's regime while at Makerere and spoke out what you believed and had to flee for your life. Despite the fact that you were in exile you achieved great success as professor at Nairobi and could have stayed there but you felt that you should return to help Uganda first as professor, then in high positions abroad as ambassador. Both in speaking and writing you said what you believed, such as your view that capital punishment should be abolished in Africa.

Contrary to what many others do, having achieved great success, you always recognised the roots of your background in Ankole. You have published folk tales, proverbs and clans and now are working on a dictionary of criminology (I would be glad if you sent me some of it). You always think of yourself as a Munyankore and have tried to set young people in Ankole to think about serious matters, particularly about Africa.

You have always been a teacher wherever you are. It is through you that I developed a great interest in Africa. In conversations here, I often refer to you as my "African brother". I have tried to get people to understand the problems that Africa has faced after colonial rule. When people refer to the violence in Africa I have called their attention to what has been happening in Ireland and the "cleansing" that went on in Yugoslovia of the Muslims and Albanians. In one incident, 7,000 people were massacred.

You have always spoken of the importance of education and have tried to get others to recognise this in both Uganda and Africa. You have established the school which I have seen growing and appreciate very much.

I can really feel that you must have a great personal impact on the students and that hopefully many will become leaders in Uganda. "You better shape up" is your motto I am sure.

All of your books have helped Africa and others to deal with crime and other problems.

My fond regards to your wonderful Muko who has played a wonderful, supporting role in your career.

Professor Marshall B. Clinard
University of Wisconsin, Madison, 2007

A

A fortiori: Latin for "from the stronger".

A priori: Latin, which means, "from what is before", used to describe an argument that proceeds from cause to effect; or from an assumption to its logical conclusion.

Ab ovo: Latin "from the egg", meaning from the beginning.

Ab initio: Latin for "from the beginning". If a marriage is unlawful *ab initio,* it means it never had validity.

Abandonment: The act of giving up a legal right, particularly a right of ownership of property. When property is abandoned, it no longer belongs to anybody and a person who takes possession of such a property acquires a lawful title to such a property. Abandonment is also an offence in the case of a parent or guardian of a child leaving the child to its fate. A child is not said to be abandoned if the parent approves steps taken by another adult to care for such a child.

Abatement: The proportionate reduction in the payment of debts that takes place if a person's arrest is insufficient to settle with his/her creditors in full.

Abduction: The law in Uganda states: "Any person, who by force compels or by any deceitful means induces, any person to go from any place is said to abduct that person."

Aberration: A departure from what is regarded as normal or acceptable or right.

Abet: To abet is to encourage or to assist, as when one assists another in the commission of a criminal act.

Abeyance: A state of temporary disuse or suspension.

Abide: To act in accordance, as to abide by the rules.

Abnormal: Any departure from the norm or the normal; abnormal behaviour is deviant behaviour, or behaviour that

1

invokes the disapproval of a significant part of the community. Examples are abundant. Homosexuality is deviant in nearly all African communities, and in many jurisdictions, it is criminal; smoking in a church is an abnormal act and therefore deviant as well; in fact the smoker could be regarded as mentally abnormal.

Abolition: From the Latin *abolitio*, which means "to abolish". The process of putting an end to the existence of a practice, an institution or custom. For example, slavery as a trade was abolished in the USA in 1863.

Abolition of Death Penalty Declaration: The declaration was made in Stockholm on 11 December 1977 by over 200 delegates and other participants from Africa, Asia, Europe, the Middle East, North and South America and the Caribbean region. The conference declared:

- The death penalty to be the ultimate cruel, inhuman and degrading punishment, which violates the right to life.
- That the death penalty is frequently used as an instrument of repression against opposition, racial, ethnic, religious and underpriviledged groups.
- That execution is an act of violence and violence tends to provoke violence.
- That the death penalty has never been shown to have a special deterrent effect.
- That the death penalty is increasingly taking the form of unexplained disappearances, extra-judicial executions and political murders.
- That execution is irreversible and can be inflicted upon innocent persons.
- That it is the duty of a state to protect the lives of all people without exception.
- That execution by government for any reason is unacceptable.
- That the abolition of the death penalty is imperative for the achievement of the desired international standards.

The conference further declared:
* Its total and unconditional opposition to the death penalty.
* Its condemnation of all executions, in whatever forms committed or condoned by governments.
* Its commitment to work for the abolition of the death penalty.

The conference concluded by calling upon:
* All non-governmental organisations, both national and international, to work collectively and individually to provide information materials directed towards the abolition of the death penalty.
* All governments to bring about the immediate and total abolition of the death penalty.
* The United Nations to declare unambiguously that the death penalty is contrary to international law (*Amnesty International Conference on Death Penalty*, 1978; Tibamanya Mwene Mushanga, *Crime and Deviance, An Introduction to Criminology*, Nairobi, 1974a).

Abortificant: Any substance that is introduced into the body orally, intravenously or otherwise with the intention of inducing an abortion.

Abortion: The termination of a pregnancy, miscarriage or the expulsion of a foetus from its mother's womb before its full gestation period is over. It is a crime to induce or to advise or assist another person to cause an abortion. In some countries, abortion may be allowed on medical advice regarding the health of the mother or when ample evidence is presented that the baby, if born, will not be able to survive. An abortion may also be procured where, owing to the mother's physical condition, there is a likelihood that irreparable damage may result from carrying the pregnancy to full term. Abortion is a crime in all countries of Latin America, but in spite of this, 35 out of 1,000 women abort each year, compared to five out of 1,000 women in the Netherlands, where abortion is legal.

Abrogation: The act of repealing a legal provision; to abolish or to annul a law.

Abscond: To travel secretly out of the jurisdiction of a court or to hide in order to avoid a legal process or to avoid arrest.

Absolute authority: Unlimited or unconditional.

Absolution: A formal release from guilt, obligation or punishment. Forgiveness.

Absque hoc: Latin which means "without this" or "if it had not been for this"; a phrase used to introduce a denial in a plea.

Abusability: A term that suggests that some children seem to invite abuse or maltreatment from their parents. Some of the common factors that appear to contribute to this situation include excessive crying, physical handicap and prematurity.

Abuse: To misuse; to insult verbally; the maltreatment of a person, especially sexually; or to assault a child. Types of abuse include sexual abuse, child abuse, abuse of office etc.

Abuse of process: An improper use of a legal process, for example to serve a summons to an individual in order to frighten him/her or to prompt a response from him/her where no suit has been filed, or filing a lawsuit for an improper purpose.

Abusing parent: A parent who is in the habit of abusing his or her own child. There are no biological characteristics by which an abusing parent can be identified except that such a person could have been abused as a child. Examples include having sexual intercourse with their immature daughters.

Abut: To adjoin; to touch boundaries; to border on.

Accede: To agree or accept; to subscribe to a treaty or agreement.

Acceptance: A voluntary act of receiving something or of agreeing to certain terms. In contract law, acceptance is consent to the terms of an offer, which creates a binding contract.

Accession: Legal acquisition by an owner of something added to his/her property; coming into possession of a right or office.

Accessory before and after the fact: An accessory before the fact is a person who aids or assists another person in the performance of a criminal act. He/she is also known as an "accomplice". In most countries, the accessory before the fact is subject to the same penalty due to the individual who performs the criminal act. An example is the twins at Ishaka Hospital in Ankole. A betrothed girl became pregnant by a man other than her fiancé. She pretended to be ill and said she was going to hospital for treatment. Her mother accompanied her. At the hospital she delivered premature twins. With the support of her own mother, she removed the premature babies from the hospital against all medical and nursing advice. On their way home, they conspired to abandon the twins in the bushes in order to conceal the birth of the babies. They hid the infants in the grass. The next day workmen found one infant alive. The mother of the twins was arrested, together with her mother, and the High Court found both women guilty of the crime of murder. Many legal systems consider concealment of the birth of a baby a crime. For instance, Section 218 of the Tanzanian Penal Code states that:

> A person who, when a woman is delivered of a child, endeavours, by any secret disposition of the dead body of the child, to conceal the birth, whether the child died before, or after its birth, is guilty of a misdemeanour.

In the case of the twins, the grandmother was an accomplice or an accessory both before and after the fact. The facts of this case rest on the destruction of the babies. Tanzanian law states that:

> A person who receives or assists another who is, to his knowledge, guilty of an offence, in order to enable him to escape punishment, is said to become an accessory after the fact to the offence. A wife does not become an accessory after the

fact to an offence of which her husband is guilty by receiving or assisting him in order to enable him to escape punishment; or by receiving or assisting, in her husband's presence and by his authority, another person who is guilty of an offence in the commission of which her husband has taken part, in order to enable that person to escape punishment; nor does a husband become an accessory after the fact to an offence of which his wife is guilty by receiving or assisting her in order to enable her to escape punishment.

In most legal systems, punishment for "accessory after the fact" is usually less than that of the principal offender and in some, it is also less than that of being an accessory before the fact.

Accident: An incident that was unforeseen and hence unpredicted, or whose causes are unknown; for example a motorist, quite unaware that there is a small child behind his/her motor vehicle, reverses the vehicle and runs over the child. This is an accident in that the motorist had no intention whatsoever to harm the child.

Accrue: To accumulate, become due as interest added to principal. Accrued interest is the interest that has become due.

Acculturation: The concept is currently used more in social anthropology than in sociology. It denotes a process of culture change in which more or less contagious contact between two or more culturally distinct groups results in one group taking over elements of the alien culture. Thus, it can be said, for example that the acquisition of European names by Africans, the use of English, the adoption of Christianity, and the general trend to change from African behavioural systems to European ways of life is a process of acculturation.

Acculturation must not be confused with enculturation, which is a process through which an individual acquires the cultural values of a society. Very often the term is used almost interchangeably with socialisation, but sometimes it is reserved to refer to the acquisition of a society's cultural tradition, by immigrant adults, while socialisation is applied to the acquisition of the same cultural values and traditions by young children.

The process of acculturation is closely related to the theory of culture conflict and crime as advanced by Thorsten Selin.

Accomplice: One who voluntarily joins another or others in committing a crime. An accomplice has the same degree of criminal responsibility as the person who commits the crime. He/she is also known as an aider, abettor, and an accessory.

Accuse: To initiate legal proceedings charging someone with a crime.

Accused: A person charged with a crime; a defendant.

Acknowledgement: Affirmation, admission or declaration recognising ownership; indicating authenticity, accepting responsibility, or undertaking an obligation to do something such as pay a debt.

Acquit: To set free from an accusation of guilty by a verdict of not guilty.

Acquittal: A legal finding that an individual charged with a crime is not guilty and is therefore set free.

Act: A law or statute; a determination or decision made in writing by a court, an exercise of power.

Act of God: A violent and catastrophic event caused by forces of nature, which could not be prevented or avoided by foresight or prudence.

Actio: Latin for "action"; refers to legal proceedings, a lawsuit, process, action, or permission for a suit.

Action ex delicto: A cause of an action based on a tort, i.e. a wrong or a transgression.

Actionable: Forming the legal basis for a civil action, such as a wrongful conduct.

Actuary: A person who calculates insurance and property costs, especially life insurance costs and insurance premiums.

Actus reus: An illegal act; it can be an affirmative act such as taking money or shooting someone dead; or it can be failure to act, for example failure to take proper precautions while driving a motor vehicle.

Ad damnum: Latin for "to the damage", the amount of damages demanded in a civil suit.

Ad hoc: Latin "for this particular purpose". An *ad hoc* committee is one commissioned for a particular purpose; for example an *ad hoc* lawyer is one designated to a particular client in a particular situation.

Ad infinitum: Latin for "to infinity".

Ad rem: Latin for "to the matter", but generally denotes that something is relevant or pertinent to the matter in hand.

Ad valorem: Latin for "to value", meaning according to what it is worth.

Addendum: Something added; a supplemental section of a document containing material added after the document had been prepared.

Adduce: To cite as an instance or as proof or evidence.

Adjournment: In court, an adjournment is a postponement or suspension of the hearing of a case until a future date. The hearing may be adjourned to a fixed date, no date could be set, or it could be adjourned for an indefinite period.

Adjudication: The formal judgement or decision of a court or tribunal.

Adjure: To put under oath; to bind a person under some penalty.

Administrative law: This is law created by administrative organs by way of rules, regulations, decisions and orders.

Admissable: Relevant and proper to be introduced in court as evidence or testimony; allowable as judicial proof.

Adopt: To agree to the formal process terminating legal rights between a child and his or her natural parents and creating new rights between the child and his or her new parents.

Adoption: The legal process by which a child-parent relationship is created between persons not related by blood. The adopted child becomes the heir and is entitled to all other privileges belonging to a natural child of his adoptive parents.

Adult: One who has attained his or her majority age of 18 and legally allowed to enter into contracts, start or defend a legal action on his or her own behalf, and to stand for public office and to vote.

Adultery: Willing sexual intercourse between a man and a woman who are not married to each other, but one of whom is married to another person. Adultery is a crime of which there is no victim in the sense that there is no complainant, since the involved persons engage in it freely and willingly. In nearly all cases of adultery, the complainant is the third party and always seek legal divorce in that capacity. In Uganda adultery is a crime punishable by 12 months imprisonment and a fine of 200 shillings and a sum of 600 shillings as damages to the husband of the wife (154 Cap.120). (In Uganda in 2006, 200 shillings could buy two eggs, and 600 shillings could buy two rolls of toilet paper).

Adversary: An opponent or litigant in a legal case.

Adverse party: The opposing party in a lawsuit.

Advocacy: The active taking up of a legal cause; the art of persuasion; a legal advocate is a lawyer.

Advocatus dioboli: Latin for "devil's advocate", a term meaning a person who deliberately opposes an argument in order to expose flaws in it.

9

Affaire: French for "business" but usually used to mean love affair; as when it is said that Mr Henda had an affair with his driver's wife.

Affiant: A person who swears out an affidavit.

Affidavit: A sworn written statement used to support applications and in some cases used as evidence in court proceedings. The person who makes the affidavit must swear or affirm that the contents are true before an authorised official such as a judge, magistrate or an advocate authorised to administer oaths.

Affirmative action: A positive step taken to correct conditions resulting from past discrimination against some class of people such as a racial group, females or religious groups.

Affray: The crime of affray is committed by taking part in a public fight or riot, which is a breach of peace. In Uganda this offence is punished by one year's imprisonment (79 of Cap. 120).

Against the evidence: A determination by a trial judge rejecting the jury's verdict that it is against the clear weight of the evidence presented or that it is based on false evidence, or may result in the miscarriage of justice.

Age and crime: Criminologists have, for some time, concluded that age is correlated with crime everywhere; and that its effects on crime do not depend on other demographic correlates of crime. Regardless of economic status, marital status, race, sex, religion and so on, younger people commit crime more often than older persons.

Age of consent: The age at which a person is legally competent to give consent, especially to marriage or to sexual intercourse. In many jurisdictions, this is set at 18 years of age.

Age of majority: The age when a person is considered legally responsible for all his or her activities and is entitled to all legal rights held by citizens in general. For example, being able to marry, to sue or be sued in court, to enter into business contracts and to stand for elective office and to vote.

Agency: A relationship in which one person, the agent, acts on behalf of another (the principal) with the authority of the latter.

Agent: One who is authorised by another person to act on that person's behalf.

Agent provocateur: Someone who incites others to commit crimes. Usually it is someone who is sent incognito by a government or the police to associate with a group of people suspected of organising a criminal or anti-government programme in order to obtain more information leading to their arrest.

Aggravated assault: An unlawful attack by one person upon another for the purpose of inflicting severe or aggravated bodily injury or by means likely to produce death or great bodily harm.

Aggression: This includes all acts of hostility, injury, violence or extreme self-assertion. Theories to explain why people become aggressive range from biological, instinctual and sociological to environmental in genesis.

The sociological approach stresses the individual's relationship with the social environment. This theory includes a frustration-aggression explanation, which states that aggressive behaviour results when purposeful activity is blocked. Sigmund Freud showed that frustration resulting from the blockage of pleasure-seeking and pain-avoiding activities leads to aggression towards the source of the obstacle or may be displaced towards another unrelated object. Another theory states that aggression is a product of socialisation and social control, which leads an individual to behave in a violent manner even when there is no frustration. In international law, aggression is the use of armed force by one state against the sovereignty, territorial integrity, or political independence of another state in violation of the charter of the United Nations; such acts include invasion, attack, military occupation, bondardment, blockade, sending armed forces to carry out violent acts in another state etc. (Buss, 1961; Marshall, 1998).

Akrasia: Greek meaning "bad mixture", "ill-tempered", "lacking in self-control", "inconsistent" and "immoderate". It is a condition in which one knows what should or must be done but is unable to do it; lack or weakness of willpower.

Alias: Latin for "otherwise", an assumed name, for example Kato Kabayo alias Butsya Nibwira.

Alibi: Latin meaning "elsewhere", a defence in law by a defendant that, at the time the crime is alleged to have been committed, the accused was not at the scene of the crime, that he or she was somewhere else. For example, the prosecution may allege that the victim was raped in Kampala on 6 January 2006; the defendant may say that he has proof to show that on that particular day he was in Kigali, and could not have committed the crime.

Alien: One who is not a citizen of a country in which he lives. An alien may be granted permanent resident status without being given citizenship.

Alienation: In sociology, alienation refers to a feeling of non-involvement in and estrangement from one's society and culture. The values and social norms shared by others seem meaningless to the alienated individual, thus the individual feels isolated and frustrated. Alienation also refers to a feeling of powerlessness. The individual gives up when he/she feels unable to control his/her own destiny or to have any significant effect on the important events of the world through his/her actions. Meaninglessness and powerlessness are both important aspects of alienation but some sociologists stress one more than the other. In ordinary social situations the two states tend to reinforce each other. Meaninglessness refers to alienation from cultural values and conduct norms, while the feeling of being powerless involves alienation from social roles, but the meaninglessness of norms leads to lack of concern for the proper performance of roles, and conversely alienation from roles necessarily results in the rejection of the norms and values that support those roles. Alienation is used in various forms in philosophy, theology, law and economics. The leading scholars on alienation have been George Hegel, Karl Marx, Ludwig Feuerbach and Sigmund Freud.

Alimony: Payment ordered by court to be made to one's estranged spouse in the case of divorce or separation.

Allegation: A statement of facts in a pleading; where the party making the allegation has the duty to adduce evidence in support of it at a trial.

Allocution: The right of a convicted person to address court before sentence is passed.

Altruism: A culturally transmitted social behaviour in which an individual demonstrates commitment to the interest of others to personal concern. The opposite of altruism is egoism, selfishness and individualism. There are indications of a hereditary element in altruism, and that it may be one of the basic elements of human nature. Assistance to offspring, relatives and kin cannot be considered as altruistic, but donating blood, contribution to charity and willingness to help even strangers is altruistic. Emile Durkheim showed that altruism is a result of over-integration in the cultural group, which may lead to suicide in which an individual takes his life as a result of over-concern for his/her community (Durkheim, 1897).

Ambiguity: Uncertainty in meaning. In legal documents ambiguity may be patent or latent.

Amicus curiae: Latin for "friend of the court", usually a lawyer who provides information for the assistance of the court.

Amnesty: A general pardon granted by a government to persons guilty of an offence (often of a political nature).

Anarchy: Lawlessness; political chaos or disorder; a state of a society in which there is no law and order, and no supreme power or authority.

Anger rape: A type of rape in which the offender is motivated by a desire to release pent-up anger and rage.

Animo: Latin for "intentionally"; deliberately.

Annuity: A sum of money payable annually for as long as the beneficiary lives, or for some other specified period of time, or the minority of the annuitant.

Annul: To make void; to dissolve that which was once in existence, e.g. to annul a marriage. Annulment wipes out all the marriage whereas divorce only ends the marriage from that point on and does not affect the former validity of the marriage. In law, annulment is a declaration by court that the marriage was never legally valid.

Annulment: An act that legally makes an act void retroactively.

Anomie: From a Greek word *anomos* which means "without law", a state of affairs in which there is absence, breakdown, confusion or conflict in the normative system of a society. Anomie is a theory that points to social disorganisation that gives rise to crime, alcoholism, vagrancy, drug addiction, hooliganism, suicide, mental disorders and deviant behaviour in general (Durkheim, 1897; Clinard, 1964).

Answer: The defendant's principal pleading in response to the plaintiff's complaint. The answer must contain the denial of all the allegations the defendant wishes to dispute as well as any affirmative defences by the defendant and any counter-claim against the plaintiff.

Anthropology: Anthropology is the study of man. It is a very broad discipline comprising such branches as:

Cultural anthropology, which deals with the biological and cultural development of man; physical anthropology, which concentrates on the anatomical and physiological aspect of man; social anthropology, which deals with patterns and principles which govern human relations; and archaeology, which is a study of antiquities or of the prehistoric remains of man and of man-made artifacts.

Anthropology in Africa is regarded as the study of what are called the primitive societies, while sociology is regarded as a study of industrialised (sometimes called advanced, developed, western, etc.) societies. Some define anthropology as the study of simple societies while sociology is the study of complex societies. This is in one respect very erroneous, as anyone who has come to be acquainted with such societies as of the Maasai, Turkana, Baganda or Zulu will have noted that these are in fact more complex than the Germans, the English and the French societies. Among the former, social relations are extremely complicated and elaborately observed, while among the latter, relations are contractual and relatively simple and in some cases temporary. Technology is simple among the former and complex among the latter. Social anthropology and sociology cover a large part of the social, economic, and political aspect of the study of human groups (Hubel, 1966).

Antisocial behaviour: Antisocial behaviour is any behaviour deemed to be against the interests of the group. It is any behaviour that is disruptive or potentially disruptive of the smooth functioning or survival of a group, regardless of whether or not group members recognise that the group's welfare is threatened. In this sense antisocial behaviour may be determined by outside observers and may include behaviour which is accepted by group members.

Apology: A defence in an action of unintentional defamation, where the defendant innocently and without negligence defamed the plaintiff but has offered a suitable correction and apology and has paid compensation. In some cases, the willingness of the defendant to offer an apology may be taken into consideration in mitigating costs for damages.

Appeal: At the trial level, if the defendant is found guilty, he or she has a right to appeal against the judgement to a higher court but not the highest court.

Appearance: The requirement of coming to court by either the plaintiff or defendant in an action, in person or through his or her attorney. The appearance in court represents a voluntary submission to the jurisdiction of the court.

Apportion: To divide fairly or proportionately and according to the parties' respective interests.

Appraise: To make an estimate of property; to assess.

Apprehension: Arrest or seizure; taking into custody of a person to answer a criminal charge.

Appropriate: To obtain a part for a particular purpose or use; it also means to wrongfully use or take the property of another.

Arbiter: Latin for "referee". A person (other than a judicial officer) appointed by a court to decide a controversy according to the law. Unlike an arbitrator, an arbiter needs a court's confirmation for his or her decision to be final.

Arbitration: A system of setting disputes by submitting them to the judgement of a mediator acceptable to both parties. An arbitrator may be an independent individual, or a committee often made up of members nominated by both parties under the chairmanship of a neutral person. Parties to a dispute usually accept the results of an arbitrator rather than face the delays, costs and risk involved in resorting to legal action.

Argument: A process of reasoning intended to establish a position required to bring about some understanding or agreement.

Arraign: To call a person to appear before court and answer charges against him.

Arraignment: The defendant is called to the bar of the court by his/her own name, the indictment is read to him/her and the court asks him whether he/she is or is not guilty. The defendant is then permitted to plead to the indictment; he/she may accept the indictment by pleading guilty or by pleading not guilty.

Arrears: A sum of money that is unpaid, although due to be paid. One who is in arrears is one who is behind in his/her payment; for example Okello is in arrears if he has not paid his rental money for the last six months.

Arrest: The apprehension of a person suspected of having committed an offence. Most arrests are carried out by police officials, with or without a written arrest warrant issued and signed by a magistrate or judge. The warrant must be shown and read to the person being arrested but not necessarily at the time of arrest. Under certain conditions, any person may arrest another person suspected of having committed a criminal act; he or she must be handed over to the police as soon as it is practicable.

Arson: A wilful or reckless, intentional destruction of property such as a dwelling structure by fire. Unlawfully, commonly destroyed property include houses, schools, motor vehicles, churches, water craft and any other property that is capable of being consumed by fire.

Artifice: A fraud or a cunning device intended to accomplish some wrong; usually it refers to craftiness or deceitfulness.

As is: A term common in commercial dealings denoting agreement that the buyer will accept and take delivery of goods in the conditions in which they are found on inspection prior to purchase, even if they are damaged or defective.

Asportation: The felonious removal of goods from the place where they were deposited.

Assassination: Intentional killing of a high-profile political or religious leader for political reasons. History repeats itself with the assassination of political leaders, some of whom include president Abraham Lincoln of the U.S. on 14 April

1865; Patrick Lumumba, former prime minister of Congo on 7 January 1961; U.S. president John F. Kennedy on 22 November 1963; Dr Martin Luther King of the U.S.A. on 4 April 1968; president Cysrian Ndaryamura of Burundi; Hendrik Verwoerd 6 September 1966; and Juvenal Habyarimana of Rwanda on 6 April 1994.

Assault: An intentional or reckless act that causes someone to be put in immediate fear of physical harm. Mere words cannot constitute an assault, but pointing a lethal weapon, such as a spear, a panga or gun is an assault, even if the weapon does not come into contact with the assaulted person. A more serious form of this crime is aggravated assault which, in the majority of jurisdictions, carries a heavier penalty.

Assess: To determine the value or the worth of something; to appraise the value of an item or something.

Assessor: A person called in to assist a court in trying a case requiring specialised technical knowledge.

Asset: Anything that is capable of being owned that has monetary value, such as a piece of land, a building etc.

Asset, fixed: This refers to property that is used for production of goods and services, such as a plant and machinery, mineral resources as well as land and buildings.

Assizes: Sessions or sittings of the criminal court.

Association: An organisation in which a group of persons joined together for a certain purpose. The purpose could be of short or long duration, e.g. a political party, a football team, a religious association. An association is to be contrasted with a community of which one finds himself or herself a part, such as a tribal, linguistic or racial group, e.g. the Chinese community, the Ismaili community or the Nubian community.

Asylum: A shelter for the unfortunate or afflicted. Political asylum is an arrangement whereby a state accepts to give shelter to a non-citizen who is fleeing from his/her country for political reasons; for example, during the reign of terror by Idi Amin in Uganda from 1971 to 1979, thousands of Ugandans had to flee Uganda and seek safety in Kenya, Tanzania and other countries.

At law: In accordance with the law; or as the law states or rules.

Atavistic: According to Cesare Lombroso (1835 – 1909), the primitive physical characteristics that distinguish born criminals from the general public. Lombroso's theory states that the characteristics of criminals are throwbacks to animals or primitive people. Lombroso held that crime was inherited and that criminals could be identified by physical characteristics.

Atrocious: An atrocious act demonstrates depraved and insensitive brutality and exhibits a senselessly immoderate use of extreme violence for a criminal purpose.

Attachment: A court order for the detention of a person and/ or his or her property. The most common attachment is the attachment of someone's earnings, by which a court orders the payment of judgement debts and other due court orders by direct deductions from the debtor's earnings. Payments are made in instalments by the debtor's employer to the court.

Attempt: An overt act, beyond mere preparation; moving directly towards the commission of a criminal offence. The attempt to accomplish a criminal offence is in itself a crime, quite separate and distinct from the crime that is attempted.

Attest: To affirm as true; to sign one's name as a witness to the execution of a document; also to bear witness to.

Attorney: An attorney is a person authorised or appointed to act in place of another person; a lawyer.

Attorney general: This is the chief law enforcement official of a government; in many countries the attorney general is also the minister of justice.

Attorney's fees: The attorney's charges for the service of representing the client.

Auction: A method of sale in which parties are invited to make competing offers or bids to purchase an item. Items commonly sold by auction by court include vehicles, buildings and land.

Audit: An inspection of the accounting records and procedures of a business, government unit or other accounting entity by a trained accountant for the purpose of verifying the accuracy and completeness of the records. Auditing may be done by a member of the organisation (internal audit) or by an independent body (external audit).

Authority: Power being delegated to a person or to a body to act in a particular way; a governing body of an organisation; a local administrative body or a town council.

Automatism: Unconscious involuntary conduct caused by some external factor. A person is not criminally liable for acts carried out in a state of automatism since his or her conduct is involuntary and therefore beyond his or her control.

Autopsy: A dissection of a dead body by a pathologist in order to determine the cause of death. This may involve the inspection of internal organs such as the heart, liver and others even by microscopic examination to determine the nature of a disease or abnormality.

B

Bad debt: A bad debt is one that is not collectable and is therefore worthless to the creditor; a debt is uncollectable because the debtor is insolvent.

Bad faith: A breach of faith; a wilful failure to respond to plain, well-understood contractual obligations; dishonesty in any business transaction.

Bail: The release of a person held in legal custody by the police, magistrate or judge while awaiting trial or appealing against conviction. There may be conditions imposed on the person on release. For example, he or she may be required to report to the police at regular intervals; he or she may be required to pay a sum of money or he/she may be required to produce people known as sureties who promise to produce the person on the day set by the court, failing which they have to pay the sum of money decided by the court. Normally bail is granted unless there is a likelihood that the person may abscond or interfere with the investigation into the case.

Bailiff: A court official who serves court orders such as summonses, writs and other court documents; he or she is also responsible for keeping order in court and directs and arranges the seating of witnesses and other court attendants, and guards the jury.

Balance sheet: A financial statement that gives an accounting picture of property owned by a company and of claims against the property on a specific date.

Ban: A formal or authoritative prohibition, e.g. a ban on public gathering without police permit, or a ban on smoking in public places.

Bandit: A robber or murderer; the term is also used to refer to an anti-government activist fighting to change government leadership.

Bank: A corporation formed for financial savings and checking accounts, that issues loans and credit and deals in negotiable securities issued by government agencies and corporations. Generally, banks fall into three main categories namely savings, commercial and saving loans.

Bankruptcy: Insolvency; the inability of a debtor to pay his or her debts as they become due. It is a court of law which declares a person bankrupt and by doing so, it may order a compulsory administration of the debtors' affairs so that his/her assets can be distributed among his/her creditors. Before one is declared a bankrupt, he or she has to apply to court by what is known as a bankruptcy petition. The state of bankruptcy can only come to an end when a court issues an order of discharge.

Bar: A legal impediment, or a legal prohibition issued by an authorised official such as a magistrate or judge. To be called to the bar (in the British legal system) is to be admitted to the legal profession as a barrister.

Bargain: A mutual voluntary agreement between two parties for the exchange or purchase of specific goods. The term also implies negotiation over the term of the agreement.

Barratry: An act of accepting bribes by a judge.

Barrister: A legal practitioner who is admitted to a place at the bar. In Britain a legal practitioner has to belong to one of the four Inns of Court. These are Gray's Inn, Inner Temple, Lincolin's and Middle Temple.

Bastard: One who is born of parents who are not legally married or what the English call illegitimate. Also refers to something unusual or unauthorised.

Battered woman's syndrome: Violent attacks leading to the murder of women who have been battered by their husbands; in some cases, this syndrome is used successfully as a defence when women are tried for the murder of their husbands.

Beccaria, Cesare (1738–94): An Italian philosopher who argued that crime could be controlled by punishments severe enough to counterbalance the pleasure people derive from them.

Bedau, Hugo Adam: Was educated at the University of Redlands, Boston and Harvard University and taught at the University of Oregon in Putland, where he was born. He has also taught philosophy at Dartmouth College, Princeton University, Rutgers University and Swarthmore College. He has published a number of articles and book reviews. He is the editor of the *The Death Penalty in America* (1964).

Behaviourism: A branch of psychology that is concerned with the study of the observable behaviour of people, rather than their unconscious motives. It focuses on the relationship between particular stimuli and people's reactions to them.

Belligerence: Aggressive and warlike behaviour.

Bench: The court; the judges composing the court collectively; it also refers to the place where the judges sit.

Beneficiary: A person for whose benefit property is held in trust.

Bequeath: To dispose of property other than land by will.

Bequest: A gift of property other than land by will.

Bestiality: A criminal offence in which a human being commits an act of sexual intercourse with a beast. Commonly victimised animals include cattle, sheep, goats, dogs, pigs and even chickens. The Uganda Penal Code states that a person who has carnal knowledge of an animal commits an offence and is liable to imprisonment for life (Sect. 145 of Cap. 120).

Betting: Risking a sum of money against another's on the basis of the outcome of an unpredictable event such as a race or a game of chance. This is not very much different from gambling, which, in some states, is illegal.

Beyond reasonable doubt: The evidence required in a criminal case for conviction, in the absence of which the accused should be left alone. The concept also refers to a state of affairs where there is no uncertainty; the facts presented to the judge or jury are sufficient to lead the judge or court to the conclusion that the defendant did commit the offence for which he or she is being accused.

Bid: An offer by an intending buyer of goods or services at a price as stated.

Bigamy: A crime which is committed when a person goes through the marriage ceremony when he or she is legally married to someone else. The only defence one can avail himself or herself is to prove to court that he or she genuinely believed that his or her spouse was dead; or that their marriage had been annulled, dissolved or was void. In many countries it is permissable to plead that one's spouse had been missing for a period of seven years and was therefore presumed dead, even when there is no proof of the death of the missing spouse.

Bill of rights: A formal declaration of the fundamental freedoms on rights of individuals commonly found in modern constitutions.

Bind over: A court order that a defendant be placed in custody pending the outcome of a criminal proceeding against him or her. He/she may thereafter be released on bail, or on other conditions of release.

Binding: Obligatory.

Blackmail: A crime of making an unwarranted demand with menace for the purpose of financial gain for oneself or someone else on financial loss to the person threatened.

Blameworthiness: The amount of culpability or guilt a person maintains for participating in a particular criminal offence.

Blameworthy: Deserving blame.

Blasphemy: An offence of reviling or ridiculing an established religion and the existence of God.

Blue collar crime: Blue collar crime is that kind of crime occurring among what are called blue-collar workers, such as semi-professional skilled and semi-skilled workers, who include plumbers, motor mechanics, carpenters, TV, radio and watch repairers, drivers etc. A building constructor may mix cement in the ratio of one to eight instead of one to four, thereby saving cement which he may sell elsewhere for his own financial benefit.

Bodily harm: An offence, inflicting any injury on another human being.

Bon avocat, mauvais voisin: French for "a good lawyer is a bad neigbour".

Bon voyage: French for "good wishes for a safe and pleasant journey".

Bona: Latin for "good"; also means virtuous, goods or property.

Bona fide: Latin meaning "in good faith"; genuine, without any element of dishonesty or fraud.

Bona vacantia: Latin which refers to goods that have no legal owner. In Latin it means "ownerless goods".

Bon vivant: French for "good living".

Bond: A written document indicating that a defendant or his or her sureties will assure the presence of the defendant at a criminal proceeding, and if not, he or she will forfeit the security posted for the bond.

Borstal: A system of juvenile treatment aimed at separating young offenders from adult and hardened offenders. It is a form of reform school that started in England in 1902. Reform schools such as the one at Kampiringisa aim at individualised rehabilitative effort during and after release from the institution.

Bot: Under the British legal system bot refers to the restitution paid by an offender to the victim.

Bourgeoisie: In Marxian theory the owners of the means of production; the capitalist ruling or middle class; the exploiters.

Boycott: To refrain from commercial or any other undertaking or dealings with someone by concerted effort; to persuade someone to refrain from doing business with someone else.

Brain drain: A neo-colonialist process whereby highly qualified persons from the Third World are lured into leaving their country and seek employment in America and Europe in order to keep the Third World countries, especially those of Africa, in a state of dependence perpetually. The most commonly lured professionals include doctors, engineers, accountants, teachers, managers and lawyers.

Branding: Marking of offenders was a common practice in Europe, the criminal being marked on the face with the first letter of his crime, for example, a rapist would have the letter "R" branded on his face, a thief would have "T" and so on. The letter was engraved on the face with hot metal.

Breach: The breaking of the law or contract; a violation or infringement.

Breach of contract: An actual failure by a party to a contract to perform his or her obligation under that contract or an indication of his or her intention not to do so.

Breach of promise: Breaking a promise which may constitute a breach of contract, for example the breach of a promise to marry may constitute grounds for a suit for damages.

Breach of the peace: The conduct that destroys public order and tranquility, including acts or words that would likely lead to violence in others.

Breaking and entering: A person commits a crime of breaking who breaks any part, whether external or internal, of a building, or opens by unlocking, pulling, pushing, lifting, or any other means whatever, any door, window, shutter, cellar flap or other things, intended to close or cover an opening in a building, or an opening giving passage from one part of a building to another. A person is legally deemed to enter a building as soon as any part of his or her body or any part of any instrument used by him or her is within the building. Punishment for "housebreaking" in East Africa is seven years.

Breath test: A test of the breath of a driver whom the police suspect of having committed a driving offence because of having been drunk, in order to determine the level of alcohol in his/her blood. There is a level of alcohol in the blood beyond which one is not allowed to drive a motor vehicle.

Breathalyser: A device by which a driver can be tested to determine the amount of alcohol in his/her body to make his/her driving of a motor vehicle dangerous to him/herself and to other road users.

Bribery: Offering, giving, soliciting or receiving something of value in an attempt to influence the action of a person in a position of trust, for instance a public office.

Brothel: A house, room or place used for the purpose of male or female prostitution. It is a crime for someone to help or manage a brothel or for a tenant or occupier of any premises to permit such premises to be used as a brothel.

Brutalisation effect: The belief that executions for criminal offences actually increase murder rates because it raises the general violence level in society and because violence-prone people identify with the executioner and not the target of the death penalty.

Buggery: Another name for sodomy, which is anal intercourse of a man with another man, a man with a woman or a beast. In the sociology of crime and deviance, sodomy and buggery are synonymous with homosexuality.

Bugging: Electronic surveillance.

Burden of proof: The duty of a party to substantiate an allegation in an issue either to avoid a dismissal of that issue early in the trial or to convince the court of the truth of that claim and hence to prevail in a lawsuit.

Burglary: The unlawful entry of a structure to commit a felony or theft; in law, the use of force to gain entry is not required to qualify an offence as burglary.

Bulletproof: Something is said to be bulletproof if it is resistant bullet penetration. A bulletproof jacket is designed to protect an individual from being hurt or even killed by bullets.

Byelaws: Also spelt bylaws; rules and regulations made by a local authority like a district council or a corporation for the purpose of regulating the conduct of members. These rules may be subject to judicial control.

Bystander: One who stands by and watches as an act is in progress; for example, one may stand by and watch as two men fight. A bystander very often becomes involved in a criminal act, either as a victim or a witness.

C

c/f: An abbreviation for "carried forward".

CIA: An abbreviation for Central Intelligence Agency, a spy agency of the United States of America.

CID: An abbreviation for Criminal Investigation Department, a branch of the police force in Uganda.

Calumny: Slander; defamation; false prosecution; false accusations.

Cannabis: A drug obtained from the crushed leaves and flowers of the hemp plant known as *Cannabis sativa*. The use of this drug is prohibited in many jurisdictions.

Cannibalism: Eating of human flesh. The practice is found among certain peoples in various regions of the world. In East Africa, the practice is virtually unknown outside the world of magic and witchcraft. In other parts of Africa, where it occurs it is usually related to ritual prescription for sacrifice.

Capital offence: An offence that is punishable by death, such as defilement, murder or treason in Uganda.

Capital punishment: Also known as the death penalty. Historically, the death penalty has been used by courts or rulers to punish a variety of crimes, some major, while others have been minor. The most common crimes punished by death include murder, rape, robbery, general theft, blasphemy, treason and heresy. People who support the abolition of the death penalty are called abolitionists, while those who uphold the death penalty are referred to as retentionists. Arguments in favour of the death penalty include:

1. The death penalty is a deterrent; its abolition will unleash dangerous elements now restrained by fear of death.
2. People who are condemned are those who are beyond rehabilitation.

3. The death penalty is less costly to the taxpayer than life imprisonment.
4. Life imprisonment as an alternative to the death penalty is inhuman.
5. By abolishing the death penalty, law-enforcement officers, especially police and prison guards, would be in danger of being killed by these dangerous persons. Because of imminent fear of being attacked, police and prison guards would be prone to kill prisoners on the slightest suspicion and thereby create a vicious circle.
6. If the death penalty were to be abolished, society would resort to lynching of even petty offenders.
8. God, in Genesis 9:6, says that "Whoever sheds man's blood, by man shall his blood be shed", meaning that God approves of the death penalty.

On the other hand, abolitionists argue that:

1. The death penalty is not a punishment at all.
2. The death penalty has been proven to have no deterrent value.
3. The use of the death penalty for murder is illogical since pure murders are really very few compared to other capital crimes.
4. The death penalty is contrary to the Christian teaching of "Thou shalt not kill", a command which applies to the state as well as to individuals.
5. The hanging of criminals is a reference to the primitive past, a symbol of imperfection and a sign of the hypocrisy of political elites in society.
6. The death penalty brutalises the society that practises it and those who carry it out. It is thus an evil that should not exist in a modern society.
8. There have been cases of the wrong person being executed, and once done, an execution cannot be reversed (Sellin, 1967; Mushanga, 1974a; Bedau, 1964).

Career criminal: A person who has repeated experience of law-breaking behaviour and has organised his or her lifestyle around criminality; someone who has made criminality a career, a life-long profession.

Careless (inconsiderate) driving: A motoring offence in which the driver drives a vehicle on a road or other public place without due care or attention and without reasonable consideration of other road users, thereby endangering their lives.

Car hop: A street-walking prostitute.

Carnal knowledge: Sexual intercourse; in Uganda used to refer to sexual intercourse between an adult man and a girl who is underage, in which case it is referred to as defilement; the penalty of which, under Uganda laws, is death.

Case: A court action or suit at law; a legal dispute; a police case is a case being handled by the police while a court case is one before a magistrate, judge or tribunal.

Castration: A form of penalty for sexual offenders in which the testicles are surgically or chemically removed. It was common for Arab countries to castrate Black male slaves in order to stop them from procreating more black people in those countries.

Castration anxiety: Freud's concept: The fear experienced by a boy during the phallic stage of sexual development that his father will cut off his penis because of their sexual rivalry for the mother.

Casus belli: Latin for "occasion for war", an event that gives rise to going to war, or to justify going to war.

Causa: Latin for "cause", motive or reason; a lawsuit or case.

Causa sine qua non: Latin for "a cause without which it would not have occurred".

Cause: That which affects a law suit.

Cause of action: A claim in law and fact sufficient to form the basis of a valid lawsuit.

Causing a disturbance: An offence which is committed by molesting other people through fighting, singing, shouting or screaming or being drunk in or near a public place.

Cave quid dicis, quando et cui: Latin for "beware what you say, when and to whom".

Caveat: Latin for " let him beware".

Caveat emptor: Latin for "let the buyer beware"; under the law, it simply means that the purchaser buys at his/her own risk.

Cease and desist order: An order of a court or other body with judicial authority prohibiting a person or a group of people to whom it is directed from undertaking or continuing a particular activity or course of conduct.

Censure: A reproach or reprimand, especially that issued by a judicial or legislative body; for example, a cabinet minister may be censured by parliament for abuse of his/her position or office or for misappropriation of funds.

Certification (of a union): The official recognition of a trade union giving it the right to represent a specific bargaining unit in collective bargaining with employers.

Certiorari: A writ from a higher court to a lower court; directing that a certified record of a named case be sent up for review. This is usually done because a complainant insists that he/she did not receive justice in the lower court.

cf: Abbreviation for the Latin word *confer* which means "compare".

Charge bargaining: A negotiated process between the prosecutor and defence lawyers for the dismissal of one or more charges against the defendant in return for the defendant's plea of guilty to the remaining charge or charges.

Charity: A non-profit organisation set up and operated exclusively for charitable, religious, educational, literary, scientific or like purposes. Contributions to such institutions are made by individuals, other institutions and business concerns. In some cases, a government may make a contribution to such an institution when it deems it necessary to do so.

Chattel: An item of personal property; any kind of property except real estate.

Chi tace confessa: Italian for "who keeps silence, confesses" meaning that someone who keeps silence accepts guilt.

Child abuse: This is an act of molestation of minors by parents or others. When the molestation is of a sexual nature the offender may be accused of indecent assault or gross indecency with children. Child abuse of a sexual nature is an offence that is not always reported to the police, but which is widely committed, remains undiscovered and may continue until the child is of an age either to be able to resist it or to report it.

Child destruction: An act causing the death of a viable unborn child during the course of pregnancy or birth. A foetus is said to be viable, that is capable of being born, if the pregnancy has lasted at least 24 weeks. If the act is carried out for a reason other than saving the life of the mother the penalty is life imprisonment in some jurisdictions.

Child support: The money that court orders one spouse to pay the other, who has the custody of the child or children born of their marriage. This may be imposed with or without alimony.

Chose: French for "a thing".

Circa: Latin for "surrounding", generally used to mean "in the neighbourhood of " or almost, or approximately, around, about (usually used for dates).

Circumstantial evidence: Also known as indirect evidence; evidence from which the court may infer the existence of a fact in issue but which does not, by itself, prove the existence of a fact directly.

Citation: An order issued by the police to a suspected offender to appear before a magistrate or judge for a minor offence; this is usually done to avoid physical detention in custody of a suspect.

Cite: To summon; to order to appear, as before a tribunal; to make reference to a text, statute, case or other legal authority in support of a proposition or argument.

Civil action: A lawsuit that deals with private or civil rights and obligations.

Civil death: A convicted person is said to be civilly dead when most of his or her civil rights, such as the right to vote, to marry or be married, to sue or to be sued, to run for elective office, have been proscribed.

Civil law: Part of the law that pertains to suits other than criminal practice and is concerned with the rights and duties of persons in contracts, torts, etc.

Claim: An assertion of a right to money or property.

Classical theory: A theoretical perception which suggests:

1. People have a free will to choose to commit crime or not to commit crime;
2. People commit crime for reasons of personal desire or greed; and
3. Crime can be controlled by intensifying fear of penal sanctions.

Classification of crimes: In East Africa, the classification of crimes was inherited from the English legal system.

First, there is the broad classification of all cases that might be tried or adjudicated by a given jurisdiction, into civil and criminal cases. Both these groups of cases are determined under two branches of law. Civil cases are dealt with by civil law. Civil law deals with property disputes between individuals or groups, and disputes about boundaries, debts, bridewealth, inheritance, purchase and matters relating to barter and exchange. Very often it is referred to as Roman Law, in contrast to English Common Law. According to English usage, a crime is an offence against the state, while a violation of the civil law is commonly known as a "tort". Assault occasioning actual bodily harm or aggravated assault may be considered as an offence against an individual (the person whose ear is cut) and also against the state, and therefore is either a tort or a crime or (very often) both, depending on the way the case is charged. Usually such a case is handled as a crime, and is tried under the criminal law procedure, and when fully adjudicated – for instance, the accused is found guilty – the assaulted person (who appears as a state witness) may proceed to bring a civil case against his assailant for damages.

Thus, a crime is a public offence, i.e. an offence against criminal law, while a tort is a wrong against a private individual. In some countries, two court systems exist to deal with these cases: a criminal court for crimes, and a civil court for civil cases; and nowadays there are traffic courts to process traffic offences such as driving a vehicle in dangerous mechanical condition; and juvenile courts for hearing and dealing with cases committed by juveniles, that is, persons below the legal age as stated by respective penal codes.

Secondly, there is a distinction between a felony type of offence and a misdemeanour. The penal code defines a felony as "an offence which is declared by law to be a felony or, if not declared to be a misdemeanour, is punishable, without proof of previous conviction, with death or with imprisonment with hard labour for three years or more". A misdemeanour is defined as "any offence which is not a felony". Both felonies and misdemeanours may be described as offences; for both types are crimes, the difference between the two being one of degree or seriousness of the offence. Thus, while the cutting and severing of a person's arm is a felony, the cutting of the same arm by making a minor incision in the skin is a misdemeanour.

It must be noted, however, that different legal systems define these two terms differently; the most useful distinguishing element being not so much the seriousness or the gravity of the offence, but the type of punishment each offence calls for. The punishment for a felony is usually specified in a penal code; for instance, Section 131 of the Penal Code of Tanzania stipulates that "Any person who commits the offence of rape is liable to be punished with imprisonment for life with or without corporal punishment."

The punishment for a misdemeanour may or may not be specified.

Clinard, Marshall Barron (b. 1911):

He is an American professor emeritus of sociology, University of Wisconsin, Madison; widely known for his contribution in the field of criminology, deviant behaviour and anomie. His books include *Sociology of Deviant Behaviour,* which first appeared in 1957. Subsequent editions were co-authored with Robert F. Meier and the book is now in its 10th edition. An equally classic work of Professor Clinard is *Corporate Crime,* with Peter C. Yeager. First published in 1960s, it resulted in an equally important work, together with Daniel J. Abbott, *Crime in Developing Countries: A Comparative Perspective,* published in 1965. Research for this book was done in Uganda.

Cocaine: A drug derived from coca or prepared synthetically, used as a local anaesthetic and as a stimulant.

Code: A systemic compilation of laws relating to an aspect of the legal justice system, such as the criminal code or penal code, motor vehicle code, etc.

Co-defendant: A defendant who is joined together with one or more other defendants in a single action.

Cogito, ergo sum: Latin for "I think, therefore I am".

Cognisable: Within the jurisdiction of the court; interest is congnisable in a court of law when that court has the power to decide the controversy; recognised.

Cohabitation: The act of living together; living together as husband and wife; having sexual intercourse.

Collateral: In commercial transactions, collateral refers to property offered as security and also to induce another party to lend money or extend credit.

Collusion: The making of a secret agreement with another to commit fraud or engage in other illegal activity or in a legal activity with an illegal end in mind.

Commercial law: A body of laws that concerns the rights and obligations of persons in their commercial dealings with one another.

Commission: Authority to exercise power or a direction to perform a duty, for example a commission of inquiry into the cause of violence at a university campus in which some students were injured; a fee paid to an employee or an agent for services performed, especially a percentage of a total receivable in a transaction; this differs from a salary, which is paid to an employee in a fixed amount at an agreed period, i.e. monthly.

Commitment: A judge's order directing that a person be taken to prison either to await trial or following the imposition of a prison sentence; also an order mandating a person to be confined in a medical institution.

Commitment warrant: A signed document issued by court indicating the period the prison is permitted to keep a suspect on remand beyond which his/her detention becomes illegal.

Common law: A kind of law that consists of guidelines, customs, traditions and judicial decisions used by the court for decision-making. It is contrasted to the constitution or written law.

Commutation: Reduction of a sentence in a criminal conviction; for example a death penalty may be commuted to life imprisonment. The commutation of a death sentence to life imprisonment is solely a prerogative of the head of state or sovereign.

Company: An association formed to conduct business and other activities in the name of the association; most companies are incorporated, that is they are registered and thereby become legal entities, gain legal personality.

Compensation: Monetary payment to compensate for loss or damage. In a criminal offence, a court may make a compensation order, whereby the convicted offender is required to pay compensation to the person who suffered loss, sometimes with interest. In a case where the offender is ordered to pay both a fine and compensation, the court can order that if he/she cannot pay both the fine and the compensation, he/she should first settle the compensation before the fine.

Competent: Properly and legally qualified; able; capable of understanding or acting reasonably. A criminal defendant is competent to stand trial if he/she is able to consult with his /her lawyer with a reasonable degree of rational understanding of the proceedings against him or her. An individual is competent to make a will if he or she understands the extent of his/her property, the identity of the natural objects, of his/her bounty and the consequences of making a will.

Competent court: A court which has proper jurisdiction over the person or property at issue.

Competent evidence: Evidence that is both relevant and proper to the issue being litigated.

Complainant: One who appears before a court of law or police officer alleging that a criminal offence has been committed.

Compos mentis: Latin for "mentally competent".

Compromise: The settlement of a disputed claim by agreement between the parties. Upon compromise any court proceedings are terminated, and the terms of agreement may be incorporated in a judgement by a court or tribunal.

Concealment: An act making more difficult the discovery of that which one is obliged to reveal or not to withhold, such as a bankrupt to schedule all his assets; or the failure of an applicant for an insurance policy to disclose information relevant to the insurer's decision to insure the risk.

Conclusion of law: As to a legal issue, reached by applying the rules of the law.

Concur: To agree; a concurring opinion agrees with conclusions of the majority but may state different reasons why such a conclusion is reached.

Condemn: Someone is condemned when he or she, for the commission of a crime, is sentenced to death; also, something is condemned if it is legally declared to be useless or dangerous or unsafe, for example a building or a sailing vessel.

Conditional bequest: A bequest that depends on the occurrence or on non-occurrence of a particular event.

Confession: An act by which an accused person willingly and without duress admits his guilt of the offence for which he or she is accused. Confession under duress or torture is illegal and inadmissible in court.

Conflict of interest: A situation in which regard for one duty results in disregard for another; an inconsistency between a public interest and the personal interest of a public official which arises in connection with the performance of official duties.

Conflict of laws: The body of the law that contains rules by which the court in which an action is brought chooses between the applicable law of the court's state and the differing applicable law of another jurisdiction connected with the controversy.

Conjugal: Matrimonial; the cordial relationship between husband and wife and relating to the enjoyment of rights and obligations of the married couple, including company and support and mutual respect based on love and interdependence.

Conjugal visit: A programme in which persons serving long prison sentences are allowed to visit their partners for sexual and other social contacts without supervision.

Consecutive sentence: Terms of imprisonment for more than one crime that must be served one after another; for example, if an offender is sentenced to three years for robbery, and another five years. For assault, he has to serve a total of eight years. For the same offences, if concurrently sentenced, the offender would serve only five years.

Consensus view of crime: A generally held view that crimes are acts of a minority, that the majority of a society share common ideals and work towards a common good, and that criminals engage in antisocial activities that conflict with social values and are therefore harmful to society.

Consent: Acquiescence; consent is required for making contracts, marriage and for a number of other social relations. Consent must be given freely, without pressure, duress or deception, and with legal competence and mental capacity. Sexual intercourse with a woman without her consent is rape. Children under the legal age of majority are deemed to be unable to give consent.

Conspiracy: An agreement between two or more people to behave in a manner that will eventually constitute an offence at least by one of them. For example, two people agree to break into a shop, one enters the shop and the other remains outside and receives the stolen goods. In conspiracy, the agreement *per se* is a crime, even when the action agreed upon is not carried out. For instance, it is a crime to conspire to overturn a legally constituted government, even if the conspiracy is not carried out.

Constitution: In a general sense, a constitution refers to the form of a thing. But in political science and in law, a constitution refers to the rules, regulations and practices that determine the composition of the organs of national, regional or even local governments within the state.

The constitution also defines and regulates the relationships between the state and the individual citizen or resident, on the one hand, and the relationship between different branches of the government and that between national, regional or local governments, or what are called political offices, on the other. The constitution also defines the functions of each branch of government and assigns powers to each to enable these units to perform their constitutional obligations in harmony.

This, in political science, is termed the separation of powers between the three major branches of government, namely the executive, the judiciary and the legislative (in Africa there is a tendency to add the military, as it very often plays a leading role in state affairs).

There are two types of constitution – one unwritten and the other written. It is said that Britain has no constitution, but that is misleading, for to have no constitution would be to be under the state of nature, which Britain is not. What it means is that there is no single document called the British constitution. Although there is no such document in Britain, the British have and know the rules and regulations that define the functions and powers of each of their political offices. Their unwritten constitution also defines the methods by which certain political offices are filled and how they relate to each other and how they relate to individuals within the nation.

Written constitutions are now the order of the day; practically every independent nation has a written constitution. Some constitutions are said to be rigid while others are not rigid.

Rigid constitutions are those which require very elaborate and prolonged procedures to change, while the flexible constitutions require very simple methods to change them. The executive includes the president, the cabinet, government departments and their branches all the way from the centre right down to the lowest government agent. The function of the executive is the maintenance of law and order, the provision of social services such as health care and education, and the defence of national sovereignty, national security and national integrity.

The legislature is the law-making branch of government. It is the parliament, which derives its powers directly from the constitution. It defines the rules and regulations by which other branches operate. Many countries have lower councils that define the functions and duties of regional, district or local governments.

The judiciary is the legal arm of the government, whose function is the interpretation of law and the administration of justice. The judiciary also acts as arbitrator in cases of disputes between the state or any of its organs and individuals. In many parts of the world, the army has emerged as a "fourth" branch of government, becoming involved in national politics by abrogating the constitution and setting up a government of its own. Maybe the army should be recognised as a branch of government in its own right and not a department of one of the branches (Adler, 1991; Dicey, 1885 and 1884).

Contempt of court: The wilful disobedience of a court ruling or regulations, or the wilful performance of an act that is deemed to be disrespectful by the court. Direct contempt of court occurs in the presence of the judge; while indirect contempt occurs while the judge is not present.

Contempt of court, in some societies, is either a criminal or a civil offence, depending upon the nature of the penalty. Civil contempt occurs when a person disobeys a court order. The crime of contempt of court has a very wide range of applications. Section 114 (1) of the Penal Code of Tanzania states:

Any person who:

a) Within the premises in which any judicial proceeding is being held or taken, or within the precincts of the same, shows disrespect in speech or manner, to or with reference to such proceeding, or any person before whom such proceeding is being heard or taken; or

b) Having been called upon to give evidence in a judicial proceeding, fails to attend or, having attended, refuses to be sworn or to make an affirmation, or having been sworn or affirmed, refuses without lawful excuse to answer questions or to produce a document or other thing, or remains in the room in which such proceeding is being heard or taken after the witnesses have been ordered to leave such room; or

c) Causes an obstruction or disturbance in the cause of a judicial proceeding; or

d) While a judicial proceeding is pending, publishes, prints or makes use of any speech or writing, misrepresenting such proceeding, or capable of prejudicing any person in favour of or against any parties to such proceeding, or calculated to lower the authority of any person before whom such proceeding is being heard or taken; or

e) Publishes a report of the evidence taken in any judicial proceeding which has been directed to be held in private; or

f) Attempts wrongfully to interfere with or influence a witness in a judicial proceeding, either before or after he has given evidence, in connection with such evidence; or

g) Dismisses a servant because he has given evidence on behalf of a certain party to a judicial proceeding; or

h) Wrongfully takes possession of any and or other property from a person who has recently obtained judgement from a court for the recovery or possession of such land or property; or

i)   Wrongfully retakes possession of any child from any person who has obtained the custody of such child under an order of the court; or

j)   Having the means to pay any sum by way of compensation or costs or otherwise in civil or criminal proceedings awarded against him by a primary court, wrongfully refuses or neglects after due notice to make such payment in accordance with any order for payment whether by instalment or otherwise; or

k)   Commits any other act of intentional disrespect, to any judicial proceeding, or to any person before whom such proceeding is being heard or taken, is guilty of a misdemeanour, and is liable to imprisonment for six months or to a fine not exceeding five hundred shillings.

Contra: Latin for "against"; in opposition to; in violation of; the reverse of.

Contra bonos mores: Latin for "against good morals"; generally referring to conduct that offends the average conscious and commonly accepted behaviour.

Contract: A legally enforceable agreement between two or more competent parties to do some legal act for good consideration.

Contumacy: Wilful disobedience of summons or orders of a court or overt deficiency of official authority which may lead to abuse or contempt of court.

Conviction: A declaration by a judge that after trial, the accused has been found guilty of the offence for which he or she is accused.

Cop out: To plead guilty; to withdraw, usually in return for a lesser charge.

Copyright: The exclusive right to reproduce or authorise others to reproduce artistic, dramatic, literary or musical works.

Corporal punishment: Physical punishment of wrongdoers,

e.g. by whipping. Corporal punishment is outlawed in Ugandan schools.

Coroner: A state official whose main function is to investigate deaths, either by ordering a post-mortem examination or conducting an inquest. A coroner may be a legally or medically trained person.

Corporate crime: A corporate crime is any act committed by corporations that is punished by the state, regardless of whether it is punished under administrative, civil or criminal law. Corporate crime is white-collar crime of a particular type; it is also an organisational crime, which occurs in the context of complex business relationships and expectations among board members, executives and managers as well as among corporation divisions, branches and subsidiaries (Marshall B. Clinard and Peter C. Yeager, 2006).

Corporeal: Something that has material reality; opposite of incorporeal or intangible.

Corroboration: Evidence that confirms the accuracy of other evidence.

Corruptio optimi pessima: Latin for "the corruption of the best is the worst of all". This is the offering or receiving of some benefit as a reward or inducement to sway or deflect the receiver from the honest and impartial discharge of his or her official duties. The definition of corruption must not be confined to monetary consideration alone, but must also include such conduct as demanding or offering sexual favours for promotion, for admission to colleges, or selection for government sponsorship, for transfers from unfavourable stations to more favourable ones by civil servants, etc. Defined in these broad terms corruption covers such offences as abuse of office, and bribing voters and election officials. Corruption has been, and still is, the most pernicious canker on the body politic of Africa. Transparency International has shown that African countries lead the world with regard to the prevalence of corruption. Corruption, illiteracy and poverty are the three major hindrances to socio-economic and democratic progress in Africa (Adeyemi, 1992, 2004; Heidenheimer, 1990).

Counselling: Counselling is a process of using interviews, psychological tests, guidance, and other techniques to help an individual solve his/her personal problems and plan his /her future realistically.

Counselling, non-directive: A technique used to assist an individual with a personal problem in which the counsellor does not make positive suggestions, direct the interview, or criticise the client. The client is left alone to "talk out" his/her problems and thereby clarify his/her problem, see him/herself objectively and finally solve the own problem with little assistance from the counsellor. Guidance is restricted to repeating and summarising major ideas and statements raised and made by the client.

Coup d'état: French; refers to a violent or illegal seizure of political power, a common way of changing governments in Africa.

Court: A body established by law for the purpose of administering justice by judges and magistrates. Court also refers to the hall or building in which a judge or magistrate sits to try cases.

Court martial: A court convened, usually composed of senior military personnel, for trying offences by serving military persons.

Consuetido pro lege servatur: Latin for "custom is held as law".

Coûte que coûte: French; emphasis that something is so essential that it must be done no matter how great the sacrifice.

Credit: Money due; it is also a privilege to delay payment extended to a buyer or borrower on the seller's or lender's belief that what is given will be repaid.

Creditor: One to whom money is owed by a debtor. In the legal context a creditor is one who voluntarily gives credit to another for money or other property, and one who has a right by law to demand and recover from another a sum of money on any account.

Cressey, Donald R.: Born 1919, studied at Iowa State University and obtained a PhD in 1950 at Indiana University. For many years, Cressey taught at the University of California at Santa Barbara. His specialisation in sociology was in the field of criminology and the book he co-authored with Edwin H. Sutherland, *Principles of Criminology* (1966), has become a classic. His other publications include *Other People's Money* (1953), *The Prison* (1961), and *The Functions and Structure of Criminal Syndicates* (1967).

Crime against nature: Sexual deviation, which includes sodomy, bestiality and homosexuality, considered a crime in many jurisdictions.

Crime and morality: A distinction must be made between crime and morality. Not all crimes are immoral and not all immoral acts are crimes. While crime is defined as the violation of societal rules of behaviour or the violation of the penal code, morality refers to adherence to and practice of moral or ethical values of a society. For example, it is a crime to keep a firearm without a licence but it is not immoral; and it may be considered immoral for people to engage in sexual play in public but not a crime.

Crime-class controversy: An endless debate rages to determine the relationship between crime and class. Certain crimes appear to predominate among the poor, such as stealing food and clothing, while other crimes appear to be more prevalent among the relatively better off, such as the bulk of white-collar crimes, forging cheques etc.

Crime control: This is a criminal justice model that emphasises the control of dangerous offenders and the protection of society. Its advocates call for harsher penalties, such as the death penalty and long prison sentences.

Crime of passion: A crime committed under the influence of sudden or extreme passion. The fact thtat an act was committed under the influence of sudden passion may provide a defence in a charge of murder because the crime lacks the element of premeditation which is necessary in a murder case.

Crime passionel: Denotes a crime held to have been committed as a result of extreme or uncontrollable feeling. It is used in murder cases motivated by sexual jealousy.

Crime prevention: A country's crime prevention policies should focus on, firstly, forestalling the commission of crime among the general public, and secondly, preventing repetition of the crime or recidivism. Some of the strategies for crime prevention in the sense of forestalling the commission of crime include:

1. The provision of opportunities for young adults to achieve and succeed in what they do. This concerns employment; under-employment or unemployment are conditions very conducive to criminality.
2. The family unit should be strengthened so that young people are adequately socialised or brought up to acquire law-abiding values.
3. Provision of counselling in schools and colleges to enforce family roles.
4. Drug and alcohol control should be stepped up.
5. The reduction of income disparities.
6. The police-public relationship is crucial in order for the police to do their job; if the public distrusts the police, police work is made difficult.
7. Improving detention, investigation and prosecution; making apprehension certain when a crime is committed may help in crime reduction.

8. Provision of relevant, sound and meaningful education to all.
9. Focusing on prevention of corruption.
10. The eradication of poverty, ignorance and disease will go a long way in the fight against crime and delinquency (Tibamanya Mwene Mushanga, 1974; Edwin H. Sutherland and Cressey, 1974).

Crime rate: The number of cases of crime reported to the police for every 100,000 people in a society; for example, if the crime rate is 15.5, it means that 155 cases of crime occurred for every 100,000 people per annum.

Crimes without victims: This refers to the willing exchange, among adults, of strongly demanded but legally proscribed goods or services. The commonest crimes without victims include abortion, homosexuality, drug addiction, alcoholic intoxication, smuggling of goods across international borders, and a host of driving offences such as driving without a permit etc. (Edwin M. Schur, 1965).

Criminal: A person found guilty of a criminal offence by a court; a criminal offence is any act that violates criminal law.

Criminal homicide: Refers to any human act that results in the death of another person. It must be differentiated from other forms of homicide, such as justifiable homicide, in which a person kills another one for reasons of self-defence; or when one carries out a judicial duty of executing a person who has been sentenced to death as a penalty for such crimes as murder, defilement or treason. cf. homicide (Tibamanya Mwene Mushanga, 1974).

Criminal law: Criminal law is defined as " a body of specific rules regarding human conduct that have been promulgated by political authority which apply uniformly to all members of the classes to which the rules refer and which are enforced by punishment administered by the state" (Edwin H. Sutherland and Donald R. Cressey, 1974).

Criminal stigmata: According to Cesare Lombroso (1835- 1909) criminal stigmata do not cause crime but make a criminal a recognisable type. These stigmata include asymmetrical face, excessive jaw, eye defects, large ears, receding forehead, prominent cheekbones, long arms, twisted nose, swollen lips and many others (Stephen Schafer, 1976).

Criminalistics: The science of crime detection based on the application of chemistry, physics, physiology, psychology and other sciences, handwriting, and other laboratory tests, in an effort to determine the nature either of the crime or of the suspected offender.

Criminologist: A person who specialises in the systematic study of crime, types of crime, causes of crime, criminal behaviour, social reaction to criminal behaviour, the criminal justice system, police work, legal sanction to law violation and measures for the reduction and prevention of crime.

Criminology: According to Edwin H. Sutherland and Donald R. Cressey, "Criminology is the body of knowledge regarding crime as a social phenomenon. It includes within its scope the process of making laws, of breaking laws, and of reacting towards the breaking of laws...". Criminology consists of three principal divisions, as follows: -

1) The sociology of law, which is an attempt to analyse scientifically the conditions under which criminal laws function and which is seldom included in general books of criminology.
2) Criminal etiology, which is an attempt to analyse scientifically the causes of crime; and
3) Penology, which is concerned with the control of crime. (Edwin H. Sutherland and Donald R. Cressey, 1966; Schafer, 1976; Mitchell, 1968.)

Cruel and unusual uunishment: A penalty tantamount to torture or excessive in proportion to the offence for which it is imposed, or inherently unfair or shocking to the people.

Cui bono: Latin commonly used by lawyers to mean "to whose benefit?"

Culpable: That which deserves moral blame, punishment and being at fault for having acted with indifference to consequences and to the rights of others.

Culture: In its common application and usage, culture refers to the integrated pattern of thinking, understanding, evaluation, communication, the process of interaction and the interpretation of social reality and experience of a people.

The way people behave, the way they interact and their way of life is their culture. The British anthropologist Sir Edward Burnett Taylor (1832 – 1917) defined culture as "that complex whole which includes knowledge, belief, art, moral, law, custom and any other capabilities and habits acquired by man as a member in the society."

The main point of the definition is that culture is socially acquired, being passed on from generation to generation, and not biologically inherited. In general usage, culture includes material arts or artifacts, as well as what is called adoption culture, which is a result of socialisation and education. In academic circles, adoption culture is studied in sociology, anthropology and history, while material culture is in the domain of archaeology. Culture is a relative concept which changes in time and space. The relativity of culture refers to what is and what is not accepted by one group. What is approved in one culture may be quite regarded as repugnant by members of another culture.

The writer recently (1999) observed with horror a social function called "the love parade" in Berlin, in which over a million and a half people took part. The parade involved street dancing, drinking, merry-making and walking up and down the main streets in the nude by adults. Compare this with the Europeans' expression when they see African women dancing with uncovered breasts. Culture is dynamic in the sense that what may be culturally disapproved of today may be acceptable at a later time. Some cultural values are irrational; others are detrimental to social progress, while others enhance social change. In many cases, culture is represented by civilisation. It is in this respect that confusion is created by claims of the existence of a higher and a lower culture when culture is used to refer to material artifacts. In this way, when one culture contains more sophisticated material artifacts, a fallacy is committed by thinking that the culture with more advanced artifacts is "higher" than one without such artifacts. No culture can be said to be better, or higher, or more advanced than another unless the reference is to the material culture of the societies under comparison.

It must also be pointed out that some cultural activities or acts are not only detrimental but also even harmful to the people. The case of female genital mutilation, a common practice in some Arab and African societies, is such a negative aspect of culture. Another harmful practice is that of burying a living wife at the death of her husband, or the destruction of twin babies.

Rational thinking and deliberate planning can make culture a very useful channel for modernisation and development (Taylor, 1871; Davis, 1949; Okot p'Bitek, 1973).

Culture and crime: Both culture and crime are common human characteristics, and as such there is no culture that can be said to be free from crime, as much as there can be no crime that can be committed without cultural definition, except in purely abnormal mental misconduct. The fact that there are crimes that are common in one culture and not in others is a clear example; for example the Mafia is a common criminal activity among Sicilians but is not known among other cultural groups. Cultural conflict, as Thorsten Sellin shows in some cases, leads to crime, e.g. female genital mutilation carried out in countries where it is not allowed. (See Marvin E. Wolfgang and Franco Ferecuti, 1967; and Marvin E. Wolfgang, 1968.)

Culture conflict: According to Thorsten Sellin, a condition brought about when the rules and norms of an individual's sub-culture values conflict with those of the dominant cultural group (Sellin, 1938).

Curriculum vitae (CV): Latin for "course of life", generally denotes a summary of someone's educational qualifications, where obtained, and work experience, for presentation to a prospective employer.

Cybercrime: Crime committed over the Internet. No law exists against this currently in East Africa. It may include hacking, defamation over the Internet, copyright infringement and fraud.

D

DMC: Abbreviation for "dangerous mechanical condition", commonly used in traffic offences.

Damage: Loss or harm.

Damages: A sum of money awarded by a court as compensation for a tort or a breach of contract.

Dangerous driving: This is the offence of driving a motor vehicle in such a way that the lives or property of others are put in danger. This offence includes driving a vehicle while under the influence of alcohol or any other intoxicant or drugs; it may also include disregarding speed limits and non-observance of road signs, e.g. failure to stop at traffic lights.

Dangerous weapon: Any device that has the potential to cause serious bodily harm, injury or to endanger life, such as a spear, knife, gun, hoe etc.

Dangerousness: Denotes the ranking of offenders and offences on some sort of seriousness along a violence-prone continuum. Dangerousness denotes physical violence and harm and does not refer to theft or damage to property.

Daninum absque injuria: Latin for "harm without injury"; refers to damage without the violation of law or damage caused by nature where the law provides no course of action to recover the loss.

Death penalty: see **Capital punishment**.

De bene esse: Latin for "conditionally", provisionally.

De facto: Latin for "in fact". Something existing as a matter of fact rather than as a matter of right. For example, it can be said that Mr Nzaire is the *de facto* leader of that organisation by the mere fact that he is in charge of the organisation even though he is not its leader in law or *de jure*.

De jure: Latin for "in law". According to the law, for example, it can be said that Mr Katontori is the *de jure* chairman of the association but Mr Buntu wields more power in the daily running of the business.

De mal en pis: French for "from bad to worse".

De minimis: Latin for "trifling", denoting something is too insignificant to warrant judicial attention.

De minimus non curat lex: Latin for "the law does not concern itself with very small matters".

De novo: For "a new", a second time, as though the first had never taken place; afresh.

De pis en pis: French for "worse and worse".

Deadly weapon: Any device capable of causing death or serious bodily injury, such as a pistol, a hammer, panga, spear, etc.

Death: A point when life ceases; permanent and irreversible termination of vital signs.

Death penalty: See capital punishment.

Debenture: A written acknowledgement of a debt secured only by the general credit or promise to pay to the issuer.

Debt: An obligation to pay a sum of money owed; a sum of money owed by a person or a group of persons to another.

Debtor: A person who owes a debt.

Deceit: A tort that is committed when someone knowingly or recklessly makes a false statement of fact, intending that it be acted upon by someone else and the person does act on the false statement and thereby suffers damages.

Deception: A false representation of words or conduct of matter of fact or law that is made deliberately or recklessly to another person.

Decree nisi: A provisional decree of divorce which becomes absolute after an interval, usually of about six months, after which the parties have the opportunity to show cause why the decree should not become absolute.

Decree of nullity: In relation to marriage, a judgement of the court announcing a marriage to be null of no effect as if the marriage had never been entered into. It does not denote divorce or separation.

Decree: An order or sentence of a court determining the rights of the parties to an action, for example a divorce decree.

Decriminalisation: A process whereby acts or omissions that were criminal are legalised, i.e. are removed from a list of crimes, e.g. some countries where homosexuality used to be a crime have decriminalised such acts and thereby legalised them.

Deed: An instrument in writing which conveys an interest in land (realty) from the grantor to the grantee. The main function of a deed is to pass title to land.

Defalcation: The failure of one entrusted with money to pay over the money when it is due to another; unlike misappropriation or embezzlement, which it resembles, it does not imply criminal fraud.

Default judgement: A judgement given without the defendant being heard in his own defence, because he failed to either respond to the plaintiff's action or to appear at the trial or hearing.

Default: Failure to do something required by law; usually failure to comply with mandatory rules of procedure.

Defeasible: Subject to revocation if certain conditions are not met; capable of being avoided or annulled; liable to such avoidance or annulment.

Defence of person or property: The general conditions and rules governing the use of force for defence of person or property are as follows:

1) In defence of his/her own person, a person may use such measures to defend him/herself as are reasonable, having regard to the nature of the assault.
2) A person is entitled to use all reasonable force to prevent the commission of a violent act upon another.
3) In defence of his or her personal property, a person may use all such means and force as are reasonable in all the circumstances.
4) In defence of person or property, a person is criminally responsible for any excess of force according to the nature and quality of the act, which constitutes the excess.

Defendant: One who is sued and called upon to make satisfaction for a wrong complained of by another. In criminal cases, the defendant is known as the accused.

Defence: This is a denial; an answer or plea disputing the validity of the plaintiff's case or making a total statement that would tend to render the defendant not liable upon the facts alleged by the plaintiff.

Defilement: An act of sexual intercourse with a female person below the age of 18 years. This is also known as statutory rape. Defilement is not rape of a minor because, under the law, a minor cannot give consent, whereas rape is the apparent unwillingness of a woman or female over 18 to have sexual intercourse.

Defraud: To deprive a person of property or interest, estate or right by fraud or deceit.

Deinstitutionalisation: A policy of removing as many offenders as possible from penal institutions such as prisons and reform schools, so that they are treated in the community.

Deliberation: The process by which the reason for and against the verdict are weighed by jurors; the purpose of the deliberation is to allow opinions to be changed by conference in the jury room.

Delict: A tort; a wrong or injury; any statutory violation; may also be used as default on monetary obligation.

Delinquency: It is usual to refer to this phenomenon as juvenile delinquency. In sociology, delinquency refers to a very wide range of socially disapproved behaviour, some of which are criminal and others non-criminal. The legal definition of delinquency is any criminal act such as theft, forgery, rape, murder, arson or malicious damage to property committed by a minor. Non-criminal acts that are labelled delinquent include rudeness, truancy, smoking, running away from home, lying, being disorderly, and being incorrigible (Wolfgang, Savitz, and Johnston, 1970; Amos, Manella and Southwell, 1965).

Delirium tremens: A psychiatric disorder associated with alcoholism; it is characterised by disorientation, hallucinations of vision, equilibrium, sensation and hearing; may be triggered by sudden withdrawal of alcohol.

Dementia: A progressive loss of mental abilities such as memory and orientation; it is usually to be found afflicting people in old age, and very often it is associated with depression.

Democracy: In brief, a political system which supplies regular constitutional opportunities for changing governing officials, and a social mechanism which permits the largest possible part of the population to influence major political, social and economic decisions by choosing among contenders for political office. In addition, democracy demands the separation of powers between the legislative, the executive and the judicial branches of government, a multiplicity of political parties, and transparency. Democracy cannot thrive under corruption and poverty; to try to make it do so is like trying to grow bananas in the Sahara (Seymour Martin Lipset, 1963).

Demonology: A theory advanced by religious preachers that man commits sin and crimes when possessed by the demon. Today demonology as a theory of criminality is rejected by most criminologists.

Demurral: Formal allegation that facts as stated in the pleadings, even if true, are not legally sufficient for the case to proceed further.

Denial: A contradiction or traverse; a refutation of affirmative allegations contained in the pleading of an adversary. A defendant's answer must accept, deny or state there is insufficient information upon which to admit or deny the plaintiff's allegations.

Deponent: A witness, especially one who gives information under oath in a deposition concerning facts known to him or her.

Deport: To send a person (even forcibly) back to his or her country of origin and forbid his or her return.

Depose: To give evidence in testimony, especially in response to interrogation during a deposition.

Depression: An emotional state characterised by sadness, unhappy thoughts, apathy and dejection. While sadness is a normal human reaction to stressful situations such as bereavement, sickness, loss of employment and other major losses, depression which is prolonged or unduly severe may require medical intervention by the administration of anti-depressant medication or cognitive therapy.

Derogation: Partial taking away of the effectiveness of a law, or partial repealing or abolishing of a law.

Descent: A cultural reckoning of human relationships, which in some communities determines the method of acquiring property, such as through inheritance. In some communities descent is through the male line, while in others it is through the female or matrilineal line.

Desertion: An act in which one abandons a relation or service in which he or she owes duties. In marriage, desertion refers to cessation of cohabitation by one of the parties with intent not to resume such relations, without the other party having given consent. Desertion may be a ground for divorce. In military terms, desertion is absence without leave, which is punishable under the military code of conduct.

Detective: A police officer, usually not in uniform, assigned to investigate crimes after they have been reported, to gather evidence and identify the perpetrator.

Detention: Detaining or holding a person charged with a crime following the person's arrest on that charge.

Determinism: A counter-proposition to classical theory or to demonology for explaining criminality. Determinism postulates that the socialisation process and all other social factors that impinge on the individual determine his/her personality, and in this situation, an individual has no free will or individual choice. The individual is under the influence of social forces beyond his/her control.

Deterrence: Deterrence by punishment is defined as a method of retrospective interference by holding out threats that, whenever a wrong has been actually committed, the wrong-doer shall incur punishment (Zimring and Hawkins,1973).

Detinue: An action for the wrongful detention of a personal property; may also refer to a legal claim for the recovery of the specific thing and for obtaining damages for its detention.

Development: In social science, the term generally refers to economic development, the acquisition by society of skills and technology of an industrial nature that leads to the world being divided into the First World, made up of North America, Europe, and Japan, the industrialised or developed world, and the Third World, comprising Africa, Latin America and Asia, which lack industrial technology. The Third World countries are also known as developing or underdeveloped countries.

Deviant behaviour: Generally speaking, deviance refers to those conditions, acts, or persons that are devalued by society or are simply regarded as offensive. Clinard and Meier have put forward four ways of defining deviant behaviour:

1. Statistical: Here deviance is behaviour which is not average. It is behaviour which is rare or infrequent. This perspective assumes that whatever the majority of people do or even approve of is the correct way of doing things.
2. The absolutist view, which assumes that social rules or norms are absolute and known to all members of the society; any deviation or departure from these established norms of behaviour is labelled deviance.
3. The reactionist approach, which labels any action or condition deviant by society or its agents of social control.
4. The normative approach, which defines deviance as the violation of social norms.

A norm is a standard about what human beings should or should not do under certain conditions (Marshall B. Clinard and Robert F. Meier, 1992; Frank R. Scarpitti and Paul T. McFarlane, 1975).

Deviation: In sociology deviation refers to any departure from socially accepted norms of behaviour; deviant behaviour is deviation, such as being a homosexual, a prostitute or a drunkard.

Devise: A gift of real property made by will; it denotes a bequest or legacy.

Dies non: Latin for any day of the week on which law courts do not conduct business, such as Sundays or public holidays.

Dieu défend de droit: French for "God defends the right".

Dieu vous garde: French for "God keep you".

Differential association: This is a sociological theory of crime and delinquency that was outlined by Edwin H. Sutherland in

1930. Sutherland held that criminal and delinquent behaviour can be explained in two ways.

The first is to consider the processes, operating at the moment of the occurrence of crime; and the second is to consider the processes operating in the earlier history of the criminal. In the first case, the explanation is called mechanical, situational or dynamic; and in the second case, the explanation is called historical or genetic. In general, sociologists have focused on the genetic explanation of criminality and delinquency. The genetic theory of criminal behaviour refers to a process by which a particular individual comes to engage in criminal behaviour. Sutherland listed nine statements in the general theory of criminal behaviour.

1. Criminal behaviour is learned. This means that criminal behaviour is not inherited and therefore a person who is not trained in crime cannot invent criminal behaviour.

2. Criminal behaviour is learned in interaction with other persons in a process of communication.

3. The principal part of the learning of criminal behaviour occurs in intimate personal groups. This means that impersonal media such as movies and magazines play a relatively marginal role in the learning of criminal behaviour.

4. When criminal behaviour is learned, the learning includes the techniques of committing the crime and specific direction of motives, drives and rationalisations and attitudes.

5. The specific direction of motives and drives is learned from definitions of legal codes as favourable and unfavourable.

6. A person becomes a criminal because of an excess of definitions favourable to the violation of the law over definitions unfavourable to the violation of law; and this is the principle of differential association. People become criminals because of this constant contact with criminal

patterns and because of their isolation from anti-criminal patterns.

7. Differential association may vary in frequency, duration, priority and intensity. This means that association with criminal behaviour and also with anti-criminal behaviour varies in those respects. Frequency and duration of this association are obvious; but priority is assumed to be particularly important in the sense that lawful and unlawful behaviour acquired in childhood may persist throughout adult life. Intensity refers possibly to the social and psychological personal attachment a person develops in contact with the criminal agent; the more intense the association the greater the likelihood of the person being criminal.

8. The learning of criminal behaviour by association with criminal and anti-criminal behaviour patterns involves all the mechanisms that are involved in any learning process. This means that criminal behaviour is not mere invention.

    In this regard, the present writer regards differential association as criminal socialisation, a process under which an otherwise non-criminal person is socialised progressively to acquire criminal and delinquent social behaviour.

9. While criminal behaviour is an expression of general needs and values, it is not explained by those general needs and values, since non-criminal behaviour is an expression of the same needs and values (Sutherland and Cressey, 1974; Mushanga, 1976; and Bold, 1958).

Differential opportunity: The theory states that people who perceive themselves as failures within conventional society will tend to seek alternative or innovative ways to achieve success. Those who come to the conclusion that there is very little hope of success by legitimate means may turn to illegitimate or delinquent means in order to realise similar goods enjoyed by those who go through the legitimate channels of success.

Diligence: Refers to attention to the matter at hand. Due diligence or reasonable diligence is that level of attention required by the circumstances in order to avoid liability in negligence.

Diminished capacity: In criminal law, the inability to have the state of mind, or *mens rea*, required for the commission of a particular crime. The defence of diminished capacity may lead to a conviction carrying a lesser penalty but not an acquittal.

Diminished responsibility: An abnormal state of mind that does not constitute insanity but is a special defence to a charge of murder. The abnormality of mind (which need not be a disease of mind) must impair the mental responsibility of the accused substantially for his/her acts, i.e. it must reduce his/her powers of control, judgement or reasoning to a condition that would be considered abnormal by the ordinary person. This condition may be due to disease, injury or mental sub-normality and covers such conditions as depression or irresistible impulses. If the defendant proves his/her defence, for example, the charge of murder is reduced to manslaughter, but he/she is not acquitted.

Diplomatic immunity: The freedom from legal proceedings granted to members of diplomatic missions of foreign states such as ambassadors, high commissioners and consul officials.

Direct and circumstantial evidence: Evidence offered before a court by an eyewitness, but evidence that may be inferred from a fact or a series of facts is what is known as circumstantial evidence. For example, direct evidence may indicate that Mr Matovu owned a pistol, that on the day of the crime he had it, and that the shot was fired by that pistol, but no direct evidence to show that Mr Matovu actually fired the shot. In this case the jury and court might infer thus from the direct evidence.

Directed verdict: When it is apparent that there is insufficient evidence to convict a defendant, the judge may direct the jury to return the verdict of not guilty, but the judge must never direct the jury to find the defendant guilty.

Disability: A state of being not fully able to perform all functions whether mental or physical; a lack of legal capacity such as infancy or insanity.

Disclaimer: The denial of a person's claim to a thing, though previously such person insisted on such a claim or right; renunciation of the right to posses and of claim of title.

Discreation: The freedom of a public official to make choices within the limits of his authority among possible courses of action.

Discrimination: The unequal treatment of human beings who are similarly situated. Discrimination is commonly encountered in employment, promotion, transfers, awarding of scholarships and business contracts, in admissions to colleges and other agencies and is usually based on race, sex, tribe, region, religion and age.

Disposition: The final decision of a court in a criminal proceeding to accept a plea of guilty, find the defendant guilty or not guilty, or to terminate the proceedings against the defendant.

Dispossess: To oust, eject or exclude another from the possession of lands or promises, whether by legal process or wrongfully.

Disqualification: Depriving someone of a right because he has committed a criminal offence or failed to comply with specified conditions. Disqualification is usually imposed in relation to activities that require licensing, for example in traffic offences.

Dissent: To disagree; a reasoned opinion that differs from that of the majority of the court.

Dissolution: In law, it means the end of legal existence of a corporation, whether by expiration of the charter, by court decree, act of legislature or by the decision of shareholders, or other means.

Distinguish: To demonstrate that an apparently similar case is different from the case at hand and that it is of limited value as precedent.

Distress: An act or a process by which a distrainer, without court approval, seizes the personal property of another in lieu of payment or what in law is referred to as in satisfaction of a claim; for example, someone takes his wristwatch to a repairer who repairs it at a cost; the owner does not pay and fetch his watch; and after waiting for a year, the watch repairer sells it to another person at a good price; he should then, after taking the amount due to him, give the remainder to the original owner.

Divestiture: Loss or surrender of a right, or title or interest.

Divide de impera: Latin for "Divide and rule".

Dividend: A corporation's profits or earnings appropriated for distribution among shareholders.

Divorce: The legal termination of a marriage and the obligations caused by marriage. Any party to the marriage may institute the legal process to terminate the marriage. Common grounds for divorce include adultery, bigamy, cruelty, impotence and desertion. Divorce is strictly disallowed by the Catholic Church, except under special circumstances.

DNA: abbreviation for deoxyribonucleic acid finger-printing (genetic finger-printing), which is a scientific technique in which an individual's genetic material (DNA) is extracted from cells in a sample of tissue and is analysed to produce a graphic chart that is unique to that person. The technique may be used as evidence of identity in a criminal or civil case, such as rape or disputes relating to paternity of a child.

Docendo discimus: Latin for "we learn by teaching".

Documentary evidence: A document, having legal effect, that is offered in court as evidence, but before such document is admitted as evidence; its authenticity must first be established by testimony relating to how it was produced and under what circumstances.

Doli capax: Latin for "capable of committing a wrong".

Domain: A piece of land of which someone is absolute owner.

Domestic violence: A common practice in which a person is subjected to physical violence by husband, wife, cohabitant, parent or descendant. Domestic violence accounts for a large percentage of battery, homicide and rape cases. In the Middle East, especially in Jordan and Saudi Arabia, women are frequently subjected to physical violence, which very often ends in homicide. The violence is justified as a way of defending the family in what are called defending the family honour in cases of sexual misconduct. Domestic violence includes what is known as child abuse, wife abuse and all family altercations that lead to misery and human suffering. Research in the United States shows that men are more often assaulted by their wives than is usually assumed (Eitzen and Zinn, 1994).

Domicile: An individual's permanent home or principal establishment. Residence is not domicile, one can have many residences, but domicile is a place where one has a home address and where one hopes to remain for a prolonged period.

Donation: A contribution; money given in support of a charitable cause, e.g. for orphans, schools, hospitals etc.

Donee: The person/organisation that receives a donation.

Donor: The person/organisation that gives a donation.

Double jeopardy: An act of prosecuting or punishing a person twice for the same offence; it is prohibited in many legal systems. The Uganda Penal Code states:

> A person shall not be punished twice either under this Code or under any other law for the same offence.

Dowry: The money and other property of a personal nature which a wife brings with her for her husband in a marriage.

Doyen: The doyen of a particular group of people or activity is viewed as its most distinguished member or representative by virtue of seniority, experience and even excellence.

Draft: A written order directing a named person to be paid a sum of money.

Draw: To withdraw money from an account in a bank or other depository facility.

Dre die in diem: Latin for "from day to day".

Driving while intoxicated: A criminal offence of operating a motor vehicle while under the influence of alcohol or drugs.

Drunkenness: Intoxication due to drinking an excess of alcohol; it is an offence in some jurisdictions to be drunk in public places.

Due care: A degree of care that a person of ordinary prudence and reason, or what in law is called "a reasonable man", would exercise given similar circumstances. Negligence is failure to exert due care and can lead to prosecution.

Due process of law: The rights or principles of justice gained over a long period of time of legal procedure which limit the government's power to deprive a person of his/her fundamental rights or freedoms or civil rights guaranteed by a national constitution.

Dupitante: Latin for "doubting". The term is used in law reports in relation to a judge who is doubtful about a legal proposition but does not wish to declare it wrong.

Duplicity: A technical invalidity arising from uniting two or more causes of action in one court of a pleading; or multiple defences in one place, or multiple crimes in one court of an indictment or two or more unrelated subjects in one legislative act, all of which are contrary to proper procedural or constitutional requirements.

Duress: Pressure, real or threatened physical force, put on an individual to act in a particular way. In law, acts committed under duress have no legal effect; for example, evidence obtained by duress is unacceptable.

Duty: An obligation of a person towards another; for example, a parent has an obligation or duty to care for his or her children. Duty also, in the law of taxation, refers to a levy or tax on goods imported or exported.

E

E.g. An abbreviation of Latin, *exempli gratia*, meaning "for example".

Economism: The policy of controlling white-collar crime through monitary incentives and sanctions.

Edict: An audience or proclamation having the force of a law, issued by a head of state or government as provided by a constitution.

Ego: Latin for "I" or "self". According to Freud's classical psychological theory, the ego is one of the three parts of the mind, the others being the id and the superego. The ego is the core around which all psychic activities revolve and it represents a cluster of cognitive and perceptional processors which include memory, problem-solving, reality-testing, inference-making and self-regulating, and all these are conscious processes that relate to social reality in which the ego acts as mediator between the demands of the id and regulatory function of the superego.

Egoistic hedonism: A psychological theory that all human actions is motivated by the desire to secure one's own pleasure, even if the pleasure or good of others has to be sacrificed.

Ejectment: A legal action brought by one claiming a right to possess real property against another who has adverse possession of the premises or who is a tenant who remains beyond the termination of a lease.

Elderly people and crime: People aged 55 and over also commit crime but not as frequently as younger people. Elderly people commit all types of crime ranging from homicide to shoplifting, from gambling to drug abuse. The difference between old and young offenders is that old offenders normally do not cause problems when being arrested, they do not fight back, they therefore do not use violence, nor do they tend to escape once they are in custody.

Electra complex: In psychoanalytic theory, a general term for a cluster of impulses and conflicts which occur during the phallic phase of sexual development at around age five. In girls the sexual fantasy is directed towards the father and hostile feelings towards the mother. Compare: Oedipus complex.

Element: An ingredient or factor, as in the elements of an offence.

Elite: A small group within a society, who possess power, prestige and status above others. An elite may be in the field of politics, economics, religion, culture or business. Sociologists are interested in how such small groups acquire, hold, use and monopolise power and what distinguishes an elite from the other members of society.

Elopement: An act of a girl who runs away from her home to be married without the consent or even the knowledge of her parents.

Emancipate: To set free from some control or restraint; for example the setting free of African slaves in America in January 1863 by president Abraham Lincolin.

Embargo: A prohibiting order; the suspension of a certain right; an order by government to restrain merchant vessels from entering or leaving its ports.

Embezzlement: Theft by an employee of his/her employer's money or property while occupying the position of trust. It is also an act in which one diverts another's money or property for one's own use.

Emolument: Profit delivered from office, rank, employment or labour including salary, fees and compensation.

Encroach: To intrude gradually upon the rights or property of another.

Encumbrance: A claim attached to real estate, such as a mortgage.

Endorsement: Writing one's name with or without permission on the back of a cheque or any commercial or financial document.

Endowment: A permanent fund of property or money to an institution or a person; the income from which is used to serve the specific purpose for which the gift was intended.

Enforcement judgement: A process or method by which a court order is enforced.

Enfranchise: To give a person or a group of people the right to vote in elections and also to be voted to an elective office.

Enjoin: To command, order or instruct with authority to suspend a refrain; for example, one may be enjoined or commended by court either to do or to refrain from doing a specific act.

Entrapment: To ensure; to catch a person by trickery. To induce a person to commit a crime which he/she had not contemplated in order to have him/her arrested and prosecuted. For example, the police may deliberately hide forbidden drugs in the house of a person they want to arrest; then search and discover the drugs and charge the house owner for possession of the drugs and prosecute him or her.

Epidemiology of crime: The term is borrowed from the field of public health, and in criminology is used to refer to facts regarding the numbers, location and social or economic characteristics of criminals. Epidemiological data are important in any attempt to understand and control criminality.

Epilepsy: Epilepsy is defined as a disease of the brain. It is characterised by:

a) Loss or derangement of consciousness or memory;
b) Excess or loss of muscle movement;
c) Alteration of sensation including hallucinations;
d) Other psychic traits including abnormal thought processes and moods.

There are two major types of epilepsy: petit mal and grand mal (minor illness and major illness). Onset is before the age of five, but very often at puberty and, extremely rare, after the age of 30. Males predominate, and it is estimated that one person in ten carries the genes for epilepsy. Epilepsy is not contagious as generally feared. It may be genetically acquired, and can be controlled with the use of medication.

Epilepsy can be diagnosed clinically and also by the use of EEG (electroencephalography). The EEG can also identify potential epileptics when there are no symptoms (Linford-Rees, 1967).

Equal protection: A constitutional provision requiring that the law be applied to all impartially irrespective of the social, economic or political status of the individual and with no regard to the race, region, sex or religion, of the person concerned.

Equality is equity: Derived from Latin to mean that if there are no reasons or any other basis for sharing the property, those who are entitled to it must share it equally.

Equitable distribution: A just division of property among interested parties.

Equity: Justice based on the concepts of natural reason, ethics and fairness independent of any codified body of law. Equity also means the administration of law according to the spirit and not merely the letter of the law.

Ergo: Latin for "therefore"; because; consequently, hence.

Err: To wander from the right away; to go astray; to make a mistake.

Errant: Irregular or unpredictable in behaviour.

Errare humanum est: Latin for "to err is human".

Erroneous: Involving a mistake; it denotes any departure from the requirements of the law, but does not imply lack of legal authority and does not denote illegality.

Error: A mistake; it is an act involving a departure from the truth or accuracy. In law, such as in a trial, an error of law may be the basis for the appellate court to reverse a judgement.

Esquire (or **Esq.**): a title for lawyers in Britain.

Estate: Estate applies to all property that a person owns, especially land.

Et al.: Latin *et alibi* which means "and elsewhere"; also *et alii* which means "and others".

Et alii: Latin for "and others".

Et cetera: (etc) Latin for "and others" or "and so forth".

Et non: Latin for "and not".

Et seq.: Latin for "and the following"

Et uxor: Latin for "and wife".

Ethnocentrism: A word first used by American sociologist William Graham Sumner (1840-1910) in his book *Folkways* (1906) as a technical term for the view of things in which one's own group is the centre of everything, and all others are scaled and rated with reference to it.

Euthanasia: The putting to death, as an act of mercy, of someone in considerable pain as a result of disease or other physical malady, for whom there is no hope for recovery. This practice has been allowed in certain European countries beginning with the Netherlands, but has not been allowed in Africa.

Eviction: The physical expulsion of someone from land through legal proceedings.

Evidence: Any other thing that may be presented in court to prove or disprove the existence of some facts. Evidence may consist of testimony, documents, real evidence and, under certain circumstances, hearsay. It is illegal, but unfortunately quite common, to obtain evidence by force or by threat of force or by torture. In respect of sedicious offences, the Uganda Penal Code Section 44 forbids conviction of a person on the uncorroborated evidence of one person.

Ex nilhilo nihil fit: Latin for "out of nothing, nothing comes".

Ex gratia: Latin for "out of grace". It denotes something done out of favour rather than as a required task as a right.

Ex officio: Latin "from the office"; by virtue of an office; officially.

Ex post facto laws: Laws that make crime an act long after it had been committed, or which retroactively increase the penalty for a crime. Any law that criminalises an act after it has been committed or increases the penalty retroactively is, in the majority of jurisdictions, unconstitutional.

Excise: Any kind of tax not applied to property, rent or incomes of real estate. It is a tax imposed directly and without assessment and is measured by the amount of business conducted or income received.

Exclusionary rule: This rule refers to the constitutional right of individuals to be secure in their persons, homes, papers and effects against unreasonable searches and seizures. The rule provides that any evidence obtained by illegal searches and seizures is inadmissible in criminal trials.

Exculpatory: Refers to evidence or statements that tend to justify or excuse a defendant from alleged fault or guilt.

Excuse: A defence to a criminal charge in which the accused person maintains that he or she lacked the intent to commit the crime (*mens rea*).

Execute: To complete; as a legal instrument, to perform what is legally required.

Executed: Fully accomplished or performed, leaving nothing unfulfilled; opposite of executory.

Execution: The process of carrying into effect a court's judgement, decree or order.

Executive clemency: The power constitutionally reposed in the president to pardon or commute the sentence of someone convicted by a court within his/her jurisdiction. For example, the president of Uganda is constitutionally empowered to reprieve a condemned offender by commuting the death penalty to life imprisonment.

Executory: Refers to something not fully accomplished or completed, but contingent upon the accuracy of some event or the performance of some act in the future.

Exemplary: Suitable to serve as a deterrent, i.e. exemplary damages given in a lawsuit.

Exhibitionism: Deriving sexual pleasure from exposing one's sexual organs in order to surprise or shock a stranger.

Exonerate: To set free from an accusation, especially in a criminal case.

Experientia docet stultos: Latin for "experience teaches fools".

Expressive crime: A crime that has no purpose except to accomplish the behaviour at hand; for example to shoot and kill someone for no apparent reason and at random as opposed to killing someone for monetary gain.

Expropriation: The taking over of private property for public use after payment of just compensation.

Expunge: The act of physically destroying information, including criminal records in files, computers etc.

Extenuating circumstances: Unusual factors tending to contribute to the consummation of an illegal act but over which the actor had little or no control.

Extinguishment: Discharge of an obligation or contract by operation of law or by express agreement.

Extortion: An offence which includes the illegal taking of money by anyone who employs threats or other illegal use of fear or coercion to obtain money, and whose conduct falls short of the threat to personal safety for robbery. Extortion as a felony is used interchangeably with blackmail.

Extradite: To give up a fugitive to the government within whose jurisdiction an alleged crime was committed.

Extradition: The surrender and transportation of a person accused or convicted of a crime in one state or nation by another holding the person in custody.

Extrajudicial: Beyond a court's jurisdiction; not connected with court or its proceedings.

Extra-territoriality: Latin for "outside the territory"; usually refers to laws which have effect outside the territorial jurisdiction in which they were passed.

Eyewitness: A person who can testify about what he/she has experienced by his or her presence at an event. For example, Matama is called upon to give evidence as an eyewitness by the mere fact that she was present when Nyindo set fire to Mukasa's house.

F

FBI.: Abbreviation for Federal Bureau of Investigation, a crime-investigating bureau of the United States of America. It is a branch of the Department of Justice and is charged with investigating all crimes except those assigned to other agencies.

Facilitation: A person is guilty of facilitating the commission of a crime when he or she knowingly assists a potential criminal to acquire the necessary means to commit the criminal act. For example, in the early 1970s a person walked into the police station in Fort Portal complaining that Roman Catholic missionaries were liars, and should be sent back to Rome. The police sent him away. He then went to an Indian shop and said he wanted to kill the priests because they were liars; he bought a panga from the shop and walked to Virika Roman Catholic Mission where he beheaded an elderly white Catholic brother, and brought his head to the police station. In this case, the Indian who sold the man a panga knew what he wanted a panga for, and therefore facilitated the criminal to commit the homicide act.

Factum: Latin meaning "deed"; a legal argument sent out in writing to be presented to a court, usually to an appeal court.

Factum probandum: Latin for "the fact to be proved".

Fair comment: A plea by a defendant in a libel suit that the statements made, even if untrue, were not intended to create ill will but rather to state the facts as the writer believed them to be.

Fairness doctrine: In some countries, it is a legal requirement that broadcasting stations present contrasting viewpoints on controversial issues of public importance. Two affirmative responsibilities are imposed on the broadcasting stations: one is to present adequate coverage of controversial public issues; and the other is to ensure that this programming presents differing viewpoints so that the public is fully and fairly informed.

Fait accompli: Refers to something that is already done or settled, and therefore cannot be changed. In French it means an accomplished fact.

False arrest: Uunlawful arrest; it is unlawful restraint of another's liberty or freedom of locomotion. It may be a criminal offence, or a basis for civil action or damages.

False imprisonment: An intentional, unsatisfied detention of a person when the confinement is imposed by virtue of one claiming legal authority to do so and an arrest takes place; the act will be false arrest as well as false imprisonment.

False plea: An obviously frivolous and absurd plea made purposely to vex or delay the court proceedings. False plea is also known as sham plea.

False pretence: The statutory offence of obtaining monies or property by making false representation of fact; it is also known as misrepresentation. For example, Obo shows Akiki a pair of earrings and says that they are made of gold and Akiki pays for the earrings; and on reaching home, she discovers that the earrings are not made of gold but of copper. At the time of negotiation, Obo knew very well that the earrings were not of gold but of copper, and was therefore making false representation; and if this can be substantiated, Obo can be sued for false pretence.

False verdict: A verdict that is manifestly unjust and quite inconsistent with the evidence. When such a verdict is rendered, the court can enter the judgement NOV (*non obstante veredicto*) notwithstanding the verdict.

Falsus in uno, falsus in omnibus: Latin meaning "false in one thing, false in all".

Family and crime: The family, of all social institutions, is the most common location of acts of violence. Child abuse, spousal abuse, sexual abuse, grievous assault, criminal homicide, assault and child neglect all occur within the family setting. In this respect, the family is the most violent social institution, which everybody should be aware of.

Fata morgana: "Is as much as a mirage". Something someone thinks he/she sees but which has no objective reality, usually attributed to witchcraft.

Fatwa: An Arabic word which denotes a legal opinion announced by a Muslim religious leader; for example in 1989 the Iranian religious leader Ayatollah Khomeini issued a fatwa to kill Salman Rushdie for supposedly blashemous material contained in his book *The Satanic Verses*. Rushdie had to go into hiding lest he be killed in response to the Ayatollah's fatwa.

Fault: Error; when applied to a people's conduct, fault denotes responsibility for or cause for wrongdoing or failure; but when applied to goods it denotes defect in either the quantity or quality of the goods.

Feasance: The doing or the performance of an act; the person who does or performs the act is known as feasor; the opposite of feasance is malfeasance.

Federalism: A form of government in which state power is shared between the central government or the government of the whole country, and regional governments or governments of the constituent regions of the nation. Federalism has proved to be a very effective mechanism for large and socially heterogeneous communities within a country. Examples include the USA, India, Canada, and to some extent, China. The opposite of this is centralisation.

Feeble-mindedness: A patient is said to be feeble-minded if he or she demonstrates a state of arrested mental development with an IQ (intelligence quotient) between 50 and 70; such a person may also be said to be sub-normal.

Felo de se: Latin which refers to one who commits suicide. Literally, it means one who commits a felon against himself or herself.

Felony murder: A homicide that occurs in the commission or in an attempt to commit a felony; for example Nkutu, together with Omar, break into Mugisha's garage intending to steal his car. On hearing the car being pushed, Mugisha opens the door and comes out to see what is happening, and at this juncture Nkutu discharges his pistol, intending to frighten Mugisha away, but injures him fatally. Legally Nkutu had no malice aforethought to kill Mugisha, but the malice is implied in the actor's intention to commit the felony.

Female genital mutilation: A common practice, not only in Africa but also in Arab lands, by which parts of the female sexual organs are excised, including the labia majora and the clitoris. In some cultures, instead of excision, the labia majora are infibulated or sewn together, leaving a small hole through which urine can be let out of the bladder. This practice has been proscribed in many countries, especially in Europe, following feminine appeals.

Ferri, Enrico: (1856–1929) an Italian disciple of Lombroso who is referred to by Thorsten Sellin as "one of the most colourful and influential figures in the history of criminology". He was an eminent criminal lawyer, an impressive orator, a journalist, a member of the Italian parliament, a persuasive lecturer and professor and a highly established scholar. Ferri sought to replace moral responsibility in judging crime with social accountability; arguing that without society there would be no law, and that the state and society have a moral obligation of self-preservation and therefore have to punish offenders. Ferri is regarded as the most prominent among the "holy three of criminology", the others being Cesare Lombroso and Raffaele Garofalo (Stephen Schafer, 1976).

Feud: A perpetual state of hostility between two corporate groups, marked by homicide or violence whenever members of the groups meet.

Fiat justitia: Latin for "let justice be done".

Fiat justica et ruat caelum: Latin for "let justice be done though the heavens fall", attributed to Lord Mansfield in Rex V. Wilkes.

Figutive from justice: One who commits a crime within one jurisdiction and flees to another in order to avoid arrest and prosecution after arrest.

Financial crime: An act in violation of the criminal law that is designed to bring financial gain to the offender.

Fine: A sum of money that an offender is ordered to pay on conviction. A fine is one of several penalties a court is permitted to award at conviction. The other common penal sanctions include imprisonment and probation, and in the case of capital offence, the court may impose corporal or even capital punishment. The amount an offender may be ordered to pay as a fine is fixed by law and corresponds to the offence committed.

Firearm: Any lethal weapon with a barrel that can shoot a bullet or any missile. Common firearms include shotguns, rifles and pistols, commonly known as handguns. Possession of a firearm without a licence from the police is illegal.

Fiscal: Pertaining to public finances and financial transactions or belonging to the public treasury.

Fiscal policy: The use of public finances and financial transactions to achieve desired economic and development goals.

Flight: To escape; leaving the scene of a crime by someone who feels guilt, or self-concealment in order to avoid arrest or prosecution after arrest. Also known as absconding.

Folie à deux: French for "madness of two people". It denotes a psychiatric condition in which certain symptoms of mental illness (such as delusions) coexist in two people who are closely related, such as husband and wife or brother and sister.

Forcible entry: Entry to real property owned by another against his or her will and without the authority of law by actual force.

Forensic: Pertaining to the courts of justice; it also indicates the application of a particular subject to the law. For example forensic medicine uses medical technology to solve some legal problems.

Forfeiture: The permanent loss of property for failure to comply with the law; the divestiture of title of property without compensation for default or an offence.

Forgery: The making of a false document with intent to defraud or to deceive; for example it is forgery to imitate another person's signature on a cheque in order to withdraw money from his or her bank account. Punishment for forgery, which is a felony, is imprisonment for three years.

Fornication: Free sexual intercourse between two unmarried persons. It is not a crime.

Forum: A court; a place where disputes are heard and decided according to law and justice; a place of jurisdiction.

Founder: A person who becomes the first to make a contribution in cash or in kind to establish a charitable institution, such as a college.

Frame-up: Conspiracy to incriminate someone with false evidence.

Franchise: The right of a citizen to vote and to be voted for in a public election for central, regional or local committees.

Fraud: A false representation by means of a statement or conduct made knowingly or recklessly in order to gain material advantage.

Free will: The concept of free will in philosophy refers to the idea of making uncaused, uncompelled or forced choices, or the ability and freedom to initiate uncaused activities; it is self-determination of the individual, the freedom to do what one fancies, chooses to do or not to do; to go this way or that way; the freedom to believe or not to believe; the freedom to join this association or the other; the freedom and the right to participate in this or that programme; and above all, the presence of independent thought.

In real life, two opposing features present themselves. One is the above situation in which an individual freely makes his or her choices; in the second instance one makes a certain decision, not because of free determination, but because of the influence of external factors. Baruch Benedictus Spinoza (1632–1677) says that "in the mind there is no absolute or free will, but the mind is determined to will this or that by a cause, which has been determined by another, and this last by another cause, and so on to infinity."

There are two sources of influential external factors that must be considered. One is the sociological factor, that focuses on societal influence on the individual. Rousseau (1712–78) states that man is born free, thereafter he is in chains that bind a normal individual to his or her community through the process of socialisation, education, indoctrination and training, through which he or she acquires normative, socially approved behaviour. If this is the case, that we behave or respond to situations in line with our social integration, then an individual is, in general, not solely responsible for his or her delinquency, and such misbehaviour could be an expression of the values internalised early in childhood. In this case, one has to blame the parents, family, neighbourhood or the community in which the delinquent was reared.

The second source of influence is divine determination. If all human action is caused by God, then the individual cannot be said to have an independent free will. A major problem is that if God is omniscient – i.e. all-knowing – and therefore knows beforehand as an eternal truth each act that each human being or any other earthly creature will commit, then humans cannot be said to possess the faculty of free will. If God is the cause (giver) of free will, humans cannot do otherwise than the way God knows they will, and if they act contrary to God's knowledge, then God cannot be said to be omniscient or omnipotent (all-powerful). If God knows of human actions before they are committed, including sins, and these acts and sins must occur according to God's design, humans cannot avoid acting according to God's will and in that sense humans cannot be said to possess free will. If God has complete foreknowledge of everything that will happen, and he is not only omniscient but also omnipotent, then God is the organiser of all things that happen and humans act in fulfilment of God's wishes.

It then appears that those who believe that God is omniscient and omnipotent must hold him responsible for all the evils that humans commit in this world without exception (Richard H. Popkin and Stroll, 1993; Lacey, 1996; Rousseau, 1762).

Freedom fighter: A person who takes part in resistance to an established political system.

Fresh pursuit: In criminal law, the right of a police officer to cross jurisdictional lines in order to arrest a fleeing felon; it also refers to the right of a police officer to arrest a felon without a warrant when he or she is in immediate pursuit of such felon.

Frisk: A police officer on patrol sees a person and through his experience and using his discretion suspects that a crime may be committed by suspecting that the person may be armed; he then stops the suspect and searches him.

Frivolous: Clearly insufficient as a matter of law; a claim is said to be frivolous if it is insufficient because it is not supported by the facts or because the law recognises no remedy for the claim.

Frotteurism: This is rubbing against or touching the sexual parts of another person against his or her will in a crowd, elevator or other public area.

Frustration: Frustration results from the prevention or obstruction of an individual's attempts to satisfy his or her needs or desires. The term is applied to a resulting emotional state which is characterised chiefly by anger and anxiety.

Frustration–aggression hypothesis: The hypothesis is that when a person is frustrated in the attainment of a desire he or she becomes aggressive, and if he or she cannot retaliate against the source of frustration (because he/she does not know the source, out of fear of consequences, or the like), he/she will direct his/her aggression towards a less threatening substitute person or object. Thus, a school teacher who is frustrated by her husband at home, either sexually, economically or socially, may direct her aggression (which is due to frustration) towards her pupils; a senior executive who is frustrated because he has not been promoted may direct his aggression towards his subordinates. They do this in order to relieve themselves of emotional and psychological tensions.

Furlough: Allowing a prison inmate to leave prison once or occasionally for a specified purpose other than work or study. The prisoner may be given a furlough to visit a sick relative, to attend a family funeral, or to arrange for a job if he/she is about to be discharged from prison. The leave is temporary and only for a short period of time.

G

Gag order: A court-imposed order to restrict information or comment about a case before a court. The purpose of such an order is to protect the interests of all parties and to preserve the right to a fair trial by curbing publicity likely to prejudice a jury.

Garnishee: A person who has been warned by a court to pay a debt to a third party rather than his or her creditor.

Garnishment: A court order notifying a person that property in his or her possession belonging to another party is attached pending the settlement of claims; a court order to an employer of a debtor to pay part of his or her wages to his creditor.

Gay bars: These are places of recreation which are important features of homosexual life in America and Europe. These bars cater exclusively for homosexuals and serve as meeting places where sexual contacts are made and new members are recruited.

Gemeinschaft und gesellschaft: German words which may be translated as "community and association". These words were first used by Ferdinand Toennies (1855-1936) to contrast social relationships in traditional rural societies with those of modern urban industrial societies. *Gemeinshaft* refers to intimate and positive relationship while *Gesellschaft* is seen as indifferent, impersonal and negative. In small-scale communities, people tend to know one another, and their relationships are meaningful and stable, but in large urban societies, people's relationships are more superficial, impermanent and anonymous and provide conditions for social deviance and criminality.

Gender: A relational concept that denotes the manner in which women and men are differentiated and ordered in a given socio-cultural context.

Gender and crime: Nearly all crime reports, arrest reports, and self-reporting surveys show that males commit far more crime than females; and that the rate for males in violent crime is much greater than that for females; the only crime that females commit more frequently than males is prostitution.

General deterrence: A crime-control policy that depends on fear of criminal penalties. General deterrence measures, such as long prison sentences for violent crimes, are aimed at convincing a potential law violator that the pains associated with crime outweigh its benefits.

Genocide: An intentional act aimed at the complete destruction of a national, racial, ethnic, religious or tribal group. The United Nations (UN) definition of genocide (1948 Convention) includes not only killing of the members of the group but also causing them serious physical or psychological harm, imposing conditions of life that are intended to destroy them physically or intended to prevent childbirth, or forcibly transferring the children of the group to another group. The UN definition of genocide does not include the destruction of a cultural or political group. The 1948 UN Convention on Genocide declared genocide to be an international crime, as are complicity in genocide and conspiracy, incitement and attempts to commit genocide (Martin, 1997; Mushanga,1994).

German: In law it means "whole" or "full"; a full brother is a brother-german, as opposed to a half-brother.

Gerrymander: To demarcate constituencies by creating unnatural boundaries in order to include or exclude members of a particular party with the aim of making it possible for a member or members of a particular party to be elected to office.

Good cause: Substantial or legally sufficient reason for doing something.

Good faith: The absence of intention to seek unfair advantage or to defraud another party; an honest intention to fulfil one's obligation; observance of reasonable standards of fair dealings.

Goodwill: A business asset which is intangible but a crucial feature of an ongoing enterprise. It is a product of good relationships with customers and suppliers of goods and services.

Graft: Fraudulent obtaining of public money by the corruption of a public official in the course of his or her official duties. A dishonest advantage of one person over another by reason of his or her position and influence.

Grand mal: French for "large illness", one of the two forms of epilepsy, the other being petit mal; grand mal is a much more severe type, being characterised by convulsions that affect almost the whole body. It begins with the patient falling on the ground, unconscious, with all muscles going into spasms, and even the breathing muscles; the body shakes, and the seizure ends when the patient either wakes up or goes into a very deep sleep.

Granny-bashing: A relatively less-noticed crime committed against elderly persons by their own offspring. It has been suggested that the root cause may lie within the process of child abuse. A child who is abused will grow to abuse his or her own children and, in turn, will be abused in his or her old age. Granny-bashing is also known as granslamming, and referred to as King Lear's syndrome (after an elderly character in Shakespeare's play, who was mistreated by his two daughters).

Grass eaters: An American term which refers to police officers who accept payoffs when they are engaged in their daily work where they can be solicited by members of the public; another word for corrupt police officers.

Gratis: Latin for "out of kindness" but in common English usage it simply means "free of charge".

Gratuitous promise: A person promises to do or to refrain from doing something without requiring consideration in return.

Grievance: An allegation that something imposes an illegal burden or denies some equitable or legal right, or causes injustice.

Groping: The fondling of another's genitalia clumsily for sexual pleasure.

Grounds for divorce: In general, divorce is granted for the following reasons: adultery, illegal sexual acts, conducting a form of marriage ceremony with another person, subjecting one's spouse to mental torment by cruelty, making continued cohabitation impossible, and continuous separation extending over a period of three consecutive years.

Guarantee: A pledge by a manufacturer regarding the quality or serviceability of a product – this is known as the warranty; also an undertaking to be responsible for another person's discharge of his or her obligation.

Guilty: An admission in court by an accused person that he or she has committed the offence by which he or she is charged. In a case of multiple charges, the accused may plead guilty to one or more charges but not guilty to others. A judicial finding of the accused person; the other finding being not guilty.

H

Habeas corpus: Latin for "you must have the body"; the name of a writ designed to compel the bringing of a person before a court or a judge.

Habitual criminal: Refers to a person who has almost made crime a habit; one who has been convicted on three or more crimes; a recidivist; a repeated offender.

Hammurabi code: A penal code developed in Babylon in 2000 BC, when Hammurabi was king in that country.

Harassment: An unnecessarily oppressive exercise of power; conduct motivated by malicious or discriminatory purposes; persecution of an individual by someone in a position of power for an ulterior motive, usually political.

Harbouring: Hiding a criminal or suspected criminal. This is the offence of impeding the arrest or prosecution of a suspected criminal.

Harlot: A prostitute; currently designated as sex worker.

Harmful: Causing or likely to cause harm.

Harmless: Not able or likely to cause harm; inoffensive.

Hashish: Leaves of the hemp plant, which are smoked or chewed for their narcotic effect.

Hate crimes: Hate crimes constitute a new category of crimes of violence. The violent acts are usually directed towards a particular person or a particular group of people because of their race, ethnicity, religion, gender, economic or political status. In America, Russia and Europe, hate crimes are directed at Africans, and to a lesser extent other non-whites. In North Africa, and especially in the Sudan, the violence is towards the Africans and non-Muslims, especially in Darfur province. The violent acts include open attacks on individuals. As a result many black people have been killed in USA, England,

Russia and France. Equally common is harassment of family members of the minority groups, attacks on cemeteries, churches, and business places.

Hatred: Intense dislike or ill-will against another.

Havoc: Widespread destruction; great confusion or disorder.

Hazardous: Risky, dangerous, dependant or chancy.

Hearing: The trial of a case before a court. Hearings are usually held in public, but under certain conditions, the hearings may be held behind closed doors or in camera.

Hearsay: Evidence of something a witness has heard others say.

Hearsay evidence: This is second-hand evidence and consists of oral statements of a person other than the witness who is testifying, and statements in documents offered to prove the truth of what was asserted.

Hedonism: The theory by Epicurus (341-270), a great philosopher, that the highest good in life is the absence of (a) pain, and (b) vexing pleasures that bring pain or discomfort as their consequence. That the aim of life should be a taraxia: tranquility (imperturbability) of body, mind, and spirit (Angeles, 1992).

Heir-at-law: An heir by right of blood.

Hereditament: Any property that can be inherited; anything that in the absence of a will descends to the heir in intestacy.

Heroin: A highly addictive crystalline analgesic drug derived from morphine, often used as a narcotic.

Hijacking: Seizing or exercising control of an aircraft in flight by the use or threat of force. Hijacking is prohibited under international law by the Tokyo Convention of 1963.

Hire: To enter into a contract for the temporary use of another's goods, or the temporary provision of his or her services or labour in return for payment.

Hire purchase: A method of buying goods by instalments. The buyer pays a deposit and undertakes to pay the rest over an agreed time, and when payment is completed, the buyer assumes ownership of the goods. Goods commonly bought on hire-purchase terms include motor vehicles, buildings etc.

Holograph: A document written completely by the hand of another; for example a will in the testator's own handwriting.

Homicide: The word is derived from the Latin *homo*, which means man or human, and *cide* that means to kill. In law, homicide refers to the death of a human being by the behaviour or action of another person irrespective of the reasons or the method. In criminal law, homicides are classified either as criminal or non-criminal. Criminal homicides are further categorised into:

> *Murder*, which is legally defined as the killing of a human being by another with malice aforethought expressed or implied. In law, malice means ill-will, where there is wickedness of disposition, hardness of heart, cruelty, recklesness of consequences and evil-mindness.

In some jurisdictions, murder is divided into first and second-degree categories.

First-degree murder is wilful, deliberate and premeditated killing; it is also first-degree murder to kill in the process of committing a felony.

Second-degree murder is killing of a human being feloniously and maliciously but without the specific intent to take a life.

> *Voluntary manslaughter*: This is the killing of a human being by another in a sudden heat of anger without premeditation, malice or depravity of heart.
>
> *Involuntary manslaughter*: This is the killing of a human being by another without malice, unintentionally.
>
> *Infanticide*: The destruction of a body before it is one year old by its own mother.

Homicide (ritual): This is a kind of homicide in which the victim is sacrificed to further the interests of the one offering the sacrifice; the usual motives include to heal a sick person, to ward off impending misfortune, or to increase one's income or profit, or to enhance one's political or business interests (Kabba, 2006).

Non-criminal homicides include: -

Execusable homicide: This is unintentional killing of a human being where no blame is attached to the killer.

Justifiable homicide: This is the killing of a human being which has been legally sanctioned; or the killing of a felon because he or she cannot be arrested, or when one kills in self-defence for fear of being killed or injured (Mushanga, 1974; Wolfgang, 1960; Paul Bohannan (ed.) *African Homicide and Suicide*, 1960).

Homosexuality: A condition in which individuals more or less permanently feel an urgent sexual desire towards, and a sexual responsiveness to, members of their own sex, and who seek sexual gratification of this desire predominantly with members of their own sex. A team of psychotherapists stated: "Our findings point to the homosexual adaptation as an outcome of exposure to highly pathologic parent-child relationships and early life situations." The statement also indicates "homosexuality may represent a fear of the opposite sex as much as a desire for the person of the same sex." A generation or so ago, a study conducted in the United States of America showed that 4 percent of white male Americans were committed homosexuals and that 37 percent of all white males in that country had had some homosexual experience (Edwin M. Schur, 1965).

Honorarium: Payment made to a person for services rendered by him or her voluntarily.

Hostage: A person who is held as security; a common practice in many parts of the world where people are seized and held as hostages while their captors demand money.

Hostile witness: An adverse witness who wilfully refuses to testify truthfully on behalf of the party who called him or her. The court may allow the hostile witness to be cross-examined by the party which called him or her.

Housebreaking: Forcing one's way into the house of another; when this happens with the intention of committing another crime, the offence is called burglary.

Human rights: Human rights refer to rights and freedoms to which every human being is entitled by virtue of being a human being; the rights are not given by the state, but the protection of the rights is the main objective of the state. It is sometimes suggested that human rights are basic to natural law and as such should be enforced in international law.

The earliest document on the rights of citizens was the Magna Carta, or the Great Charter, that was extracted by the barons from King John in 1215. The Magna Carta's provisions applied to the nobles and barons, but not to common people. The US Bill of Rights of 1791 followed the Declaration of the Rights of Man and of the Citizen after the French Revolution in 1789.

The observance of human rights has passed through three stages. First was rights of a political nature, such as the right to freedom of speech, of assembly, and of religion. The second phase was economic in nature, i.e. the right to an adequate standard of living, the right to medical care, and the right to education. The third phase involved the cultural rights, such as the right to preserve one's culture, language and traditions, and environmental protection.

The Universal Declaration of Human Rights was adopted by the United Nations General Assembly in 1948. The first article states that:

All human beings are born free and equal in dignity and rights. They are endowed with reason and conscience and should act towards one another in the spirit of brotherhood.

Then, in 1966, the International Covenant on Civil and Political Rights as well as the International Covenant on Economic, Social and Cultural Rights were established.

In 1981, the African Charter on Human and People's Rights, also known as the Banjul Charter, was signed.

In addition to the above there are the Convention on the Prevention and Punishment of the Crime of Genocide (1948), the International Convention on the Elimination of all Forms of Racial Discrimination (1965) and the International Convention against Women (1979).

The United Nations set up a Commission on Human Rights which has the power to discuss gross violations of human rights but not to investigate individual complaints. In spite of the fact that conventions and declarations have been established since 1948, the abuse of human rights is still rampant in many parts of the world. In some countries, the leaders have turned human rights into a national hymn and demand the poor nations to rehearse it as conditionality before they can be given the annual handouts. Western countries, and notably the United States of America, is a leading example regarding the call for the observance of human rights in spite of the fact that its own track record in this respect leaves a lot to be desired. In many Third World countries human rights charters have largely remained on paper, as massive abuses are committed daily by state agents as a matter of routine. Destruction of and brutality towards unarmed civilians is common in the majority of nations. It is common for people just to "disappear" as if their lives had no value. During the Amin and Obote regimes in Uganda as many as one million people died and many more were forced into exile (1971–1986). The number of people who were killed during apartheid rule in South Africa and the extent of inhuman suffering will never be known.

The number of people killed in the Congo under the

murderous regime of King Leopold II of Belgium (1885-1908) has been estimated at ten million (*New Africa,* 1999); but nobody will ever knew now many people had their hands cut off as punishment for not harvesting the king's rubber crop (see Hochschilds, 1998).

The slave trade itself represented the most horrendous of all abuses of human rights. It is regrettable that certain forms of slavery still exist today in the practice of luring young women with promises of housework, only to imprison them as prostitutes in foreign countries.

Colonialism, imperialism and neocolonialism or globalisation are practices that continue to perpetuate the abuse of human rights in Africa. Even African leaders, who had themselves grown up under intolerant and abusive European regimes, the signing of the charter on Human and People's Rights in 1981 notwithstanding, are unable to respect the human rights of their people. The worst example of the gross abuse of human rights was the state-managed genocide in Rwanda in 1994.

Perhaps the urgent responsibility of African leaders is education, inculcation and internalisation of respect for human rights and reverence for all life, in order to eliminate man's inhumanity to man (Martin, 1997; Humana, 1992).

Humanitarianism: A doctrine in penal philosophy that advocates that convicts be treated humanely by prohibiting harsh, severe, painful and degrading conditions in all penal institutions.

I

I.e.: *id est*; Latin, meaning "that is".

Ibidem: Latin meaning "in the same place".

Id: Latin idem which means "the same". In Freud's theory, the id represents the most primitive reactions of the human personality, consisting of a blind striving for immediate biological satisfaction, regardless of cost.

Id est: (i.e.) Latin for "that is to say", commonly used in abbreviation as i.e.

Idem: Latin for "the same".

Ignorantia legis non excusat: Latin for "ignorance of the law is no excuse". The fact that the accused person did not know that what he or she was doing was illegal does not prevent the law from punishing him or her for the act. For example, one cannot plead not guilty to killing an animal in a game park just because one did not know that it is not allowed.

Illegal: Something is illegal if it is not authorised by law; contrary to law.

Illegitimate child: A child is illegitimate if his or her parents were not married at the time of his or her birth; in some countries such a child is called a bastard, and can only become legitimate when the parents marry.

Immaterial: What is immaterial is irrelevant in law; something is immaterial if it has nothing to do with the case before the court.

Immunity: Freedom or exception from legal prosecution. In different countries some people are excepted from legal proceedings by virtue of their constitutionally deferred statuses while they exercise their prescribed roles, such as sovereigns, heads of state, lawmakers, and judges. In nearly all countries all people with diplomatic status are immune to legal proceedings, which needs to be lifted before they can be prosecuted.

Impertinent: In law, to any pleading or evidence that is legally deemed to be irrelevant to the case before the court.

Implied consent: Consent that is found to exist solely because certain actions or signs would lead a reasonable person to believe that consent is present, whether or not that consent is specifically expressed. In criminal law, implied consent is used as a defence in rape cases if the defendant states that he acted under a reasonable and honest belief that the woman was more than willing to accede to his demands.

Impossibility: In criminal law, impossibility applies to situations in which facts or circumstances render the commission of the crime impossible. For example, Kamau could not have killed Onyango in December 2005 since Onyango had died in a car accident two months before.

Impound: To place merchandise, funds, documents or records in the custody of an officer of the law.

Imprisonment: A penal sanction in which an offender is held in prison for the length of time determined by court in accordance with the provisions of the national penal code. Imprisonment is also known as incarceration. The idea of imprisoning an offender for a crime was introduced into Africa by European colonialists. Today, it ranks highest as a penal sanction for all sorts of crimes ranging from manslaughter to theft of every description. Prisons are overflowing with criminals which, in many cases, is proving to be a glaring abuse of human rights. People are theoretically sent to prison as a punishment, but in Africa, this view is reversed, so persons are in for punishment; they are denied even the simplest right like the right to write a letter in confidence to one's friends etc.

Impute: To assign legal responsibility for the act of another because of the relationship between those made liable and the actor, rather than because of participation in or knowledge of the act.

In absentia: Latin for "in absence"; for example, someone can receive a degree or be sentenced in his or her absence.

In camera: Latin for "in the room", in common usage it means behind closed doors; not in public.

In delicto: Latin for "at fault".

In flagrante delicto: Latin for "while the crime is blazing", meaning in the very act of committing the crime; red-handed.

In toto: Latin meaning in general, on the whole.

In vino veritas: Latin for "in wine there is truth", a proverb warning drinkers that while drunk they may say what they may not have said when sober.

Inalienable rights: What are known as fundamental rights, including the right to practise the religion of one's choice, freedom of speech, due processes and equal protection of the laws; rights that cannot be transferred to another nor surrendered, except by the person possessing them.

Incapacitation: An objective of sentencing, the aim of which is to restrain a potential offender from commmitting new or different offences by holding him or her in a maximum prison from which escape is unlikely.

Incarceration: Imprisonment in a jail, prison or any penal institution for a period of time ranging from one day to a life-term imprisonment.

Incest: In anthropology, incest is a sexual relationship between persons who are members of the same culturally defined kinship group. It is an act of incest for a man to have sexual contact with his mother, daughter, grandmother, granddaughter, sister, aunt and other near female relatives. Similarly it is an incestual act for a woman to have sex with her father, son, grandfather, grandson, brother and uncle.

Incest is a crime in many countries, and though it committed frequently, it is reported infrequently. Punishment for incest is imprisonment for seven years; while incest with a person under 18 years could result in a 14-year prison sentence.

Incommunicado: Latin; if a person is held incommunicado it means that he or she is denied the right to speak to others or receive messages.

Incompetency: Disqualification or lack of a legally recognised qualification or fitness to discharge the required duty.

Indemnity: An obligation to make good any loss or damage another person has incurred or may incur. Indemnity also refers to the right of the person who has suffered loss or damage to claim restitution.

Indian hemp: A herbaceous plant, *Cannabis sativa*, native to Asia; its fibre is extracted from the stem and used to make ropes and stout fabrics.

Infanticide: The killing of a baby who is under 12 months of age by its mother. The killing of a baby by any other person, whether its father or not, is criminal homicide and is punishable like any other criminal homicide, murder or manslaughter. In the case of infanticide, if the mother can show that she was suffering from the effects of pregnancy or lactation, she may have her case reduced from murder to manslaughter and her sentence may be reduced accordingly.

Infidelity: Being disloyal to one's sexual partner by having sexual relations with a third party; unfaithfulness in sexual relations. Infidelity is a common basis for divorce, separation as well as being a common source of domestic violence, spousal abuse and homicide.

Injunction: A court order to do or to refrain from doing some act.

Innuendo: In an action for defamation, a statement in which the plaintiff explains the defamatory meaning of apparently innocent words that he or she alleges are defamatory. The plaintiff must set out in his or her pleadings the facts of the circumstances making the words defamatory.

Inquest, the coroners: A post mortem examination of a dead person conducted soon after a killing or when unexplained death occurs. The purpose of an inquest is to determine the cause of death. The coroner's report is not binding on the prosecution but serves in an advisory capacity, which the court may uphold, ignore or reject. The coroner may give the cause of death as "accidental death" but the court, which has access to more information, may find that death actually resulted from someone's criminal act, and may convict a person charged with the crime.

Insanity: In criminal law, insanity is a defect of reasoning which is a result of mental disease, which prevents a person from knowing that what he/she did was wrong. A person accused in court is assumed to be sane, that is capable of knowing what is right and what is wrong and therefore responsible for his /her acts. In law, insanity is defined in terms of the McNaghten rules. This determination includes psychoses, paranoia and schizophrenic diseases but not psychopaths, neurotics and those with subnormal minds.

Intelligence: General intelligence is the innate potentiality of an individual, which determines how educable he or she is in any direction. Intelligence determines the maximum level that he or she can attain, all things being equal. In this connection it is important to distinguish ability from capability; the former refers to potential or talent while the latter refers to mental power. Intelligence quotient (IQ) is the ratio formed by dividing mental age by chronological age and multiplying the result by one hundred.

The mental age of a person is determined by a standardised intelligence test. Social psychologists have shown that the intelligence of a person is dependent on his or her personality, willpower and social milieu, and that it is possible to relate intelligence to vocational categories as follows:

Highest professional and academic IQ 150 + , which is 0.1% of the adult population.

Lower professional and higher technical IQ 130 – 150, which is 0.3%.

Executive, general professional, highly skilled IQ 115 – 130, which is 12%.

Skilled, clerical and ordinary commercial IQ 110 – 115, which is 26%.

Semi-skilled, poorest commercial IQ 85 – 110, which is 33%.

Unskilled and coarse manual labour IQ 70 – 85 which is 19%.

Casual labour IQ 50 – 70, which is 7%.

Mentally abnormal persons IQ 50 and less, which is 0.2%.

It must be noted that the bulk of the people have an IQ of 90 to 110. These include teachers, chiefs, politicians, senior civil servants and the like (Gleitman, 1981; Linford-Rees, 1967).

Intelligence and crime: There is insufficient evidence to show that low intelligence is related to criminality; the kind of crimes that may be related to low intelligence (IQ) are those committed by people exhibiting mental abnormality or reduced responsibility.

Intention: The state of mind of one who aims to bring about a particular consequence. Intention is one of the main forms of *mens rea*. Intention is not the same as motive; intention is very often contrasted with recklessness.

Intermittent sentence: A sentence of imprisonment in which the convict is required to spend weekends and holidays in prison while he or she is free to go out and work or study on week days.

International Court of Justice: This is also known as the World Court and is the major UN judicial organ to which all member nations of the UN are party. The court consists of 15 judges who are elected for a term of nine years each by the General Assembly of the UN. Its main objective is settlement of disputes between nations, and decisions are reached by majority vote. Once a decision is made, the party that disputes the decision may appeal to the Security Council of the UN. The court is in permanent session except when on vacation; it has its seat at The Hague, the Netherlands. The World Court must not be confused with the International Criminal Court; the latter is not an organ of the UN although it also sits in The Hague *(The World Almanac,* 2005; *The World Book,* 1988).

International Criminal Court (ICC): This court was created on 17 July 1998 in Rome when 120 nations signed the statute to establish it. Its mission is to try individuals accused of genocide, war crimes or other crimes against humanity. By the end of 2005, only China, Japan, Russia and the United States had not signed the statute. The International Criminal Court is not an organ of the UN but an independent agency. It consists of 18 judges who are elected by members nations to serve three-year terms; it has a president, and first and second vice presidents; and jurisdiction is limited to member nations only *(The World Almanac,* 2005).

International law: Also known as the law of nations or, in Latin, *gentium:* The system of law regulating the interrelationship of sovereign states and their rights and duties with regard to one another.

Interpol: This is an international criminal police organisation created on 13 June 1956, the objective being to promote mutual assistance among all police authorities within the units of the law existing in different countries. Its membership stands at about 181 nations.

Intestacy: A state in which a person dies without having made a will disposing of all his or her property.

Invalid: Something that has no binding force; or without authority.

Ipso jure: Latin for "by the law itself".

J

Joint liability: Shared liability that allows a sued person the right to insist that others be sued jointly with him or her.

Joint venture: A business undertaking by two or more parties in which profits, losses and control are shared; very often the term is used interchangeably with partnership.

Judex damnatur cum nocens: Latin for "the judge is condemned when the guilty is acquitted".

Judge: A state official authorised to adjudicate on disputes and other matters brought before the court for decision. To be appointed a judge, one should be an experienced, legally qualified person; a judge is superior to a magistrate and has the power to try and decide on indictable offences.

Judgement: A decision or legal determination of a case before a court in which the accused, called the defendant, is found to be either guilty or not guilty. A judgement is usually followed by a penal sanction such as a prison term or a fine if the accused is guilty or an acquittal if found not guilty.

Judicature: The administration of justice, judges collectively, the term of office of a judge. For example, during Ugentho's judicature, he served in many parts of the country.

Judicial: Pertaining to the administration of justice; belonging to the office or status of a judge.

Jump bail: Colloquial expression meaning to leave the jurisdiction or to avoid appearing as a defendant in a criminal trial after bail had been posted, thus causing a forfeiture of bail.

Jurant: A sworn legal officer such as a magistrate.

Jure divino: Latin for " divine law".

Juridical: Relating to juridical proceedings or the law.

Jurisdiction: Refers to the powers of a court to hear and decide the case before it. That power is derived from the state organ that created the court in the first place; such organs are either the constitution or the legislature.

Jurisprudence: The philosophy or science of law; knowledge or skill in law; also the laws as set out in previous judicial decisions.

Jurist: An expert scholar of law, usually applied to those who specialise in writing on legal subjects; also refers to a judge.

Juror: A person sworn in as a member of a jury or one who has been selected for jury duty but not yet assigned a case.

Jury: A group of men and women selected at random to determine the facts of a case and give a verdict in criminal cases and occasionally civil cases. The judge has the duty of guiding the jury in matters of law, but they must be left alone to come to the decision of whether to convict or acquit the defendant. The judge must alert the jury that they alone may convict or acquit the defendant on matters of fact when duly satisfied beyond reasonable doubt. Ideally, the jury's decision should be unanimous, and it is a criminal offence to attempt to influence the verdict of a jury. However, juries are not used in all countries.

Jus: Latin for a law, right.

Jus humano: Latin for "human law".

Jus naturale: Latin for "law of nature".

Just deserts: (ironical, colloquial) An outcome in which virtue triumphs over vice.

Justice: A moral ideal that the law seeks to uphold in its protection of rights and punishment of wrongs. Justice is not synonymous with law, for law may be just or unjust. Benjamin Disraeli (1804-1881), former British prime minister, referred to justice as "truth in action" *(Oxford Dictionary of Quotations, 1980).*

Justifiable controversy: A real controversy appropriate for judicial determination, this is to be distinguished from a hypothetical dispute.

Justifiable homicide: The killing of a human being by commandment of the law, in the execution of public justice, in self-defence, in war, in rebellion and in defence of habitation, property or person.

Justification: Just and lawful cause or excuse; showing in court sufficient reason for the defendant doing what he/she is called upon to answer, so as to excuse liability.

Juvenile offender: An offender who is aged between 10 and 17 years. A young offender is aged 14 and 17; in many jurisdictions a child who is aged between 10 and 14 cannot normally be indicted for a criminal offence unless it is for homicide. In some cases, a young offender may be charged together with someone else aged 18 and above. A juvenile offender, if found guilty, may not be sentenced to death, or to imprisonment; instead he or she will be sent to a detention home or reform school.

Juvenile delinquency: Applies to a process involving young people engaged in criminal acts, that if committed by adults, would be punished by criminal processes, but because of their being minors, are dealt with differently, such as probation or referral to young offenders' corrective centres.

K

Kangaroo court: This refers to a court that has no legal authority; that disregards all the rights normally accorded to persons and whose decisions are not legally binding. The term is also used to refer to a court that is biased against a party and thus renders unfair verdict or judgement.

Keeping the peace: This is a moral as well as a legal and civic obligation to behave in such a way that one does not cause or threaten a breach of the peace, i.e. a disturbance of public order.

Kerb crawling: An offence by a man soliciting a woman for prostitution in a street or public place, either from a motor vehicle such as a taxi or a bus or just having alighted from one. The soliciting is persistent or likely to cause annoyance to the woman or a nuisance to the people around.

Kidnapping: In Uganda, the law states:

> Any person who conveys any person beyond the limits of Uganda without the consent of that person or of the person legally authorised to consult on behalf of that person is said to kidnap that person from Uganda (Sect. 239. Cap. 120).

The penalty for kidnapping in Uganda is imprisonment for ten years (Sect. 242 Cap. 120).

Kleptomania: A mental abnormality or condition that leads an individual to feel an urge to steal. The person suffering from this defect usually steals items of no or little value, such as one earring or one sock, or something that costs very little and which he or she could easily afford.

L

Labelling: This is a practice whereby a person is defined and described in terms of his or her conduct; for example a person who is seen to be drunk daily is called or labelled a drunkard; and one who has broken a law is labelled a criminal. In sociology, especially in the sociology of deviant behaviour, labelling deals with human interaction, behaviour and social control. Labelling is seen as a form of social control in that it affects both a person's self-image and other people's reaction. What is crucial is who does the labelling and whether the label sticks.

Labelling theory of criminality: An approach to the explanation of criminal behaviour that emphasises how and why an act is considered rather than looking at why the individual committed the act.

Laches: An undue delay in asserting a legal right or privilege.

Laissez-faire: French term which denotes the principle that governments should not interfere in the economic affairs of the country, but leave people to carry on their business, trade, etc. as they see fit.

Land: Real estate or real property; or any tract that may be conveyed by deed; may not only refer to the earth but also to things of a permanent nature found or affixed there.

Landlord: The owner (the lessor) of a property who leases it for a period for a stated amount to a tenant or lessee.

Larceny: The unlawful removal of someone's property with the intention of keeping it permanently; in other wards larceny is stealing and its punishment depends on the amount or value of the item and the character of the offender, i.e. if he or she is a young or first offender.

Latent defect: A defect that is hidden from knowledge as well as from sight and one that would not be discovered even by the exercise of ordinary and reasonable care.

Law: The term law, in a strict sense, means a rule to which actions conform or should conform. Laws of physical sciences refer to facts which have been proved correct and do not change over a period of time. These laws are also permanent and universal, e.g. law of motion, law of gravity, etc.

The laws of social science are those laws that establish the relationship between the cause and effect of certain facts, but these laws are true under given conditions only, e.g. the laws of economics, laws of sociology, etc. Moral laws are rules of human conduct for members of society. These laws guide people on how to live peacefully in society with other members. For instance, "do not tell lies" and "love thy neighbours" are examples of moral laws.

The laws of the state are those laws that are made and enforced by the state. It is the duty of every citizen to obey and uphold these laws. If citizens disobey the laws they will be punished for the various wrongs, e.g. theft is a crime and whoever breaks this law will be punished by the state.

Purpose of law: Each society has its laws that are created, primarily, to govern human conduct towards other humans. But the laws created may also be used to preserve the status quo in an attempt to keep peace and order. These laws are also created to provide justice to all members of that society, to protect fundamental rights and freedoms of individuals and to establish procedures and regulations regarding the daily transactions between individuals. It can thus be concluded that man-made laws are those laws that deal with freedoms of individuals and that ensure that they enjoy these freedoms and rights without interference from any other individuals or the state. For Kant "natural right rests upon pure rational principles a priori; positive or statutory right is what proceeds from the will of a legislator...Innate right is that which belongs to everyone by nature, independent of all judicial acts of experience. Acquired right is that right which is founded upon such juridical acts" (Adler, 1991).

Law and morality: Other than the laws laid down by the state and enforced by the courts, there are certain customary rules of behaviour called *rules of morality*. These are also rules or ideals which regulate conduct, by which conduct can be organised and limited. They may also be described as a set of moral conduct with a sense of fairness and justice, which humans possess by the pure activity of their power to reason. These laws, however, are not enforced in courts and depend, for their effect, solely on the force of public opinion, although many rules of morality may well be given the status of rules of law by statutes, etc and thereby become enforced by the courts. For instance, theft is against morality and also against the law. There is no necessary nexus between law and morality. The crucial difference between the rules of law and the rules of morality lies in the method of their enforcement.

There is a great deal of common ground between the law of the state and moral laws or obligations. Whereas laws of the state provide for what is accepted as reasonable behaviour in a society, moral laws state what is accepted in all societies. These moral laws can be said to supplement the laws of the state. Dennis Lloyd (1970) states that

> ...both are concerned to impose certain standards of conduct without which human society would hardly survive and, in many of these fundamental standards, law and morality reinforce and supplement each other as part of the fabric of social life... If we do not refrain from physical assault on others and from misappropriating what belongs to others there can be no security of life or of the transactions which further life and well-being in human society.

Lloyd goes on to explains.

> Moral codes, by recognising that we ought generally to refrain from such acts, supplement the force of the law which equally forbids them. And the moral reprobation which such acts inspire is reinforced by the criminal and other sanctions imposed by the law.

Types of law: Over the years, as law developed, there also arose a need to establish various principles of law and this necessitated the distinction of certain cases that involved persons only and those that involved the state. As a result, the distinction of a crime, which is a wrong by an individual against the state, and a tort, which is a wrong by an individual against another individual, developed.

There now exist various types of law that deal with various types of cases. Criminal law deals with crimes, civil law, also known as private law, deals with the relations of individuals among themselves. Civil law includes the law of contract, the law of succession, the law of torts, the law of property, the law of equity and so on. Criminal law, on the other hand, deals with the public generally, and the person who has committed a wrong against the state or a crime will be prosecuted by the state and will be dealt with by the state in the interest of the general public. For example, if a man attempted to murder his neighbour, and was arrested, he would be charged and prosecuted by the state and the neighbour or the victim will have no direct interest in the case. The neighbour may, however, sue the man in a civil court and claim compensation, but only after the criminal proceedings have ended. It is therefore clear that civil law deals with private individuals and the state has no interest in the case as long as law and order are maintained.

The punishments in civil and criminal cases also differ. In criminal law, criminals are usually punished by imprisonment whereas in civil cases, the wrongdoer is usually required to pay damages to the victim as compensation.

Common law and civil law distinction: The common law system of jurisprudence originated in England. This system of law is based on judicial precedents or previous court decisions rather than legislative enactments, such as statutes, and it is therefore derived from principles rather than formal rules. Historically, in the absence of statutory law or written law regarding a particular subject, the judge-made rules of common law became the law on the subject.

Common law evolved from generally accepted norms and customs in England. Over the years, these customs were largely accepted and they then came to be known as the common law of England. The main source of common law today, since it is an unwritten law, is through judgements of prior cases, which are usually available in Law Reports or from books of authority. The system of precedent simply means that the judges are in a position to interpret the law in situations where the facts of the case are similar to those of a previous case. The judgements from the previous case will then have to be considered in delivering judgement in the case at hand. It is, however, difficult to follow this system of law in that no two cases can have the same facts and circumstances, and also because a lower court judgement cannot bind a decision of a higher court. However, a lower court, such as the High Court, is still bound by the decision of a higher court, such as the Supreme Court. This is the basis of the system of precedent.

No matter how consistent the details of every particular case, the social and economic changes that have continued to take place also contribute to the variance in the circumstances of each case. The system of precedent, although often frustrating, is much fairer in the delivery of justice in that the judge is free to interpret a situation as he or she sees fit, unlike written laws that are usually rigid and are only amended or changed after it has proved to be unjust.

The civil law system of jurisprudence, on the other hand, differs from common law in that it originated from western Europe, mainly France, Spain, and Italy, and is used throughout the world in non-Commonwealth countries and some parts of the United States, such as Lousianna and the province of Quebec in Canada. The civil law system of jurisprudence should also be distinguished from the civil law branch of common law, which deals with private individuals.

Civil law is made up of a single integrated document, which supports an exhaustive statement of the law on the subject matter it deals with. It is also codified in that all the wrongs and their respective punishments are written down in the form of codes. For instance, the code of criminal procedure deals with crimes and their punishments, the code of commerce and so on. This system is also different in that the system of precedent does not apply and the decisions of a higher court are not binding on any other court. The judges are also highly involved in civil law cases, as they are responsible for interpreting the law and delivering judgement on the case. This is not the case in common law in the United States, for instance, where the judgement is usually reserved for a jury (Martin, 1997).

Divisions of civil law

a) Law of contract

A contract is a promise or an agreement which is legally binding or enforceable by law. The law of contract determines whether a promise or an agreement is legally enforceable and also establishes its legal consequences.

b) Law of torts

The word "tort" in French simply means "wrong". In English law, it is used to denote a wrong that is actionable at the suit of the injured party or the victim. The legal redress in the law of torts is generally the award of damages to the injured party. The law of torts may also be divided into other categories. Wrongs such as negligence, defamation, trespass and nuisance form the law of torts. It should be noted, however, that certain torts, although committed against an individual, may also constitute wrongs against the state. For instance, defamation, libel or a written defamatory statement, or cases of negligence, may constitute torts and crimes at the same time.

c) Law of property

The law of property deals with the nature and the extent of the rights which people may enjoy over land and other property. The law of property may be divided into two separate categories. On the one hand, the property in question may be in the possession of one person, who under the law has certain rights over other people. On the other hand, the owner of the property also has certain rights and privileges over other people. Equitable interests and legal interests in land are determined by whether one claims ownership or possession of the land. For instance, a mortgager and mortgagee both have different interests in the property, although one has ownership and the latter has possession.

d) Law of trusts

A trust is a relationship which arises whenever one person, called the "settlor", transfers his or her property to another person, called the "trustee" on the condition that the trustee holds that property for another known as the "beneficiary". The law of trusts deals with the various aspects of trusts and imposes a strict obligation on the trustee to administer the trust property in accordance with the conditions of the trust document.

Sources of law in Uganda

There are several avenues that constitute the formation of law in Uganda. There are also different organs through which these laws are created. It should be noted that, in order for a law to be effective and to serve its purpose, it needs to be enforced, validated and accepted in the locality. It is promulgated and publicised so that those who are subject to it can learn its provisions. It must be recognised by law enforcers, namely, the courts and police officers.

A source of law can be written or unwritten and this raises the issue of the distinction between written and unwritten laws. Some of the sources of law in Uganda include legislation or acts of parliament as well as the constitution, which may be classified as written laws. This is especially true in cases where decrees, ordinances, acts and so on are cited to enable a person to know the court's position on a given issue.

There are also foreign laws that constitute part of the laws of Uganda and these laws also have jurisdiction in Uganda, such as the general principles of family law, the law of equity and contract law, which have all been imported into Uganda, and other Commonwealth countries, and as such constitute a great portion of the laws of these countries.

Other sources of the law in Uganda include customary laws, which deal with specific cases and whose enforceability is subject to certain limitations. Customary law in Uganda only deals with land disputes involving land held under customary tenure, marriage and divorce as well as dowry issues, and other matters dealing with intestate succession of deposition of property to heirs as far as it is not governed by any written law. Other requirements that have to be met in order for customary law to be enforceable in Uganda, for instance, customary law, must not contradict written law; it only applies in civil matters, it must not be "repugnant to natural justice, equity and good conscience" and must not be excluded by the parties involved.

Other sources of law include subsidiary legislation or delegated powers of legislation, for instance bye-laws and ordinances, which are created under the Local Governments Act, case law or judicial precedents, which simply means the judicial decisions of previous courts in a case of similar facts and circumstances, and Islamic law, which primarily governs laws relating to marriage under Islamic or sharia law.

Law of the land: Rules and regulations for maintenance of law and order in society enforced by legislative authority or court decisions and those established by custom.

Lawyer: One who is qualified in law and is licensed to practise law, that is, authorised to represent another person or group of persons and legal persons such as companies before court; a lawyer is sometimes referred to as an attorney or an advocate.

Leading question: A question posed by a trial lawyer that is sometimes improper because it suggests to the witness the answer he or she is to give; or in effect it prompts answers in disregard of actual memory.

Lease: A legal agreement by which the lessor grants to the lessee the possession and use of the property for a stated period and for an agreed periodic payment called rent.

Leasehold: The estate in real property of a lessee created by a lease, generally an estate of fixed duration.

Legacy: A gift of personal property transmitted by a will; a bequest or inheritance.

Legal: Of or based on law; something concerned with law; something done in accordance with the provisions of law; for example, a marriage is said to be legal if the people involved in the marriage go through the marriage ceremony as outlined by law.

Legal duty: That which the law requires to be done or forborne.

Legalised brothels: In many countries, especially in Europe and America, prostitution is accepted as any other business enterprise and is therefore licensed. This is usually done in order to control two problems that tend to go hand in hand with prostitution i.e. the spread of venereal diseases and organised crime. In countries where prostitution is legalised, the prostitutes are expected to be examined by a physician on a regular basis; their medical report for fitness is to be displayed with a licence to practise prostitution.

Lesbianism: This is homosexuality among females. The name is derived from the Greek island Lesbos where a group of women lived, led by the poetess Sappho (born ca. 630 BC), whose sexual relations were homosexual. In many societies lesbianism is disapproved of, while in others the habit is condemned. It is said to be common in one-sex institutions such as prisons, convents and boarding schools (Clinard and Meier, 1992).

Lèse majesté: French meaning any crime against authority, especially treason.

Lethal: Something is lethal if it is deadly or fatal; for example a deadly weapon, or a fatal blow to the head.

Levy: To impose a tax or fine; also the tax itself.

Lex: Latin for "law".

Lex talionis: Retribution; the Law of Moses, which states "an eye for an eye, and a tooth for a tooth", and "a life for a life". *Lex talionis* served as a development from a vengeful law and was a restraint on wanton penalties; it sought to equate the penalty with the injury the victim had sustained and no more. It was also the basis of the code of Hammurabi of 1875 BC (Mushanga, 1974).

Liability: Responsibility by an individual or an organization either for damages resulting from a negligent act, or for an obligation, or for the payment of a debt.

Libel: A statement in written form that injures the reputation of another person; a form of defamation expressed in writing, printing or in any form of recording. Libel in Uganda is a misdeamour.

Licence: A grant of permission required to enable a person to legally do a particular thing, exercise a certain privilege or pursue a particular business or occupation. Licences may be issued by individual persons, government departments or professional bodies; for example lawyers, doctors, engineers and others need licences to be able to practise.

Licensee: One to whom a licence has been issued.

Licensor: One who grants a licence to another.

Lie detector: A machine that records emotional disturbances on a graph, the polygraph, which shows whether the person being tested is lying or not.

LIFO: This stands for "last in, first out", a rule in some businesses regarding the hiring and firing of employees.

Line one's pocket: This is a colloquial phrase used to refer to making money out of corrupt practices by persons in positions of trust.

Lineup: A police procedure in which a person suspected of having committed a crime is placed in a line together with other people so that a witness can identify the person he or she believes was one who committed the crime.

Lingua franca: Italian, meaning a language used as a means of communication, especially in trade between peoples who do not understand each other's native languages, such as Kiswahili in east and central Africa. In Italian, it originally meant the French language or Frankish tongue; today it does not refer to a national language.

Liquidate: To settle, to pay a debt; to determine the amount due, to whom due and then to extinguish the indebtedness. The term usually refers to the settlement of debts.

Lis pendens: Latin for "a pending lawsuit", which refers to the order that pending the suit nothing should be changed.

Litigant: A person who is a party to a court action. A litigant may, if he or she so chooses, present his or her case to court, or he/she may hire the services of a lawyer to represent him/her in court.

Litigation: A judicial contest aimed at determining and enforcing legal rights.

Locus: Latin for "the place".

Locus standi: Latin for "the place of standing"; but in legal parlance it means "the right to appear and be heard in court".

Loiter: To linger for no evident reason, particularly in a public place such as a market, school, bus station, etc. There are behaviours that are associated with loitering that are prohibited, such as begging, gambling, soliciting someone to engage in sexual intercourse or for the purpose of selling or smoking drugs.

Lombroso, Cesare: (1835–1909) An Italian, trained as a medical doctor, who had a very keen interest in psychology; he was later appointed professor of criminal anthropology at the University of Turin, to which he donated his brain at his death. In his early years, when he worked as an army physician, he was interested in measuring physical differences, which he related to psychological attitudes. His comparative studies of physical characteristics as related to psychological ones, led him to write a book *L'uomo delinquente* (1876).

Lombroso's general theory was that criminals differ from non-criminals in their physical characteristics of atavistic or degenerative anomalies. Lombroso's contribution to criminology has been upheld by leading scholars in this field and one of them, the distinguished American criminologist Thorsten Sellin, wrote that: -

> Whether Lombroso was right or wrong is perhaps in the final analysis not so important as the unquestionable fact that his ideas proved so challenging that they gave an unprecedented impetus to the study of the offender.

> Any scholar who succeeds in driving hundreds of fellow students to search for the truth, and whose ideas after a half a century possess vitality, merits an honourable place in the history of thought (Sellin, 1937).

Lumpenproletariat: German, first applied by Karl Marx (1818–1883) to refer to the very lowest section of society not consisting of workers but of the outcasts of society, such as tramps, beggars and thieves, who are poor, poorly dressed, ill-educated, etc.

M

McNaghten Rules: In law, insanity is defined in terms of rules, according to which, if an offender pleads that at the time of committing the criminal act he/she did not know what he /she was doing, or that if he/she knew what he/she was doing, he at the time, did not know that what he was doing was wrong then he was incapable of knowing right from wrong. In East African countries, the law in force provides that:

> A person is not criminally responsible for an act or omission if at the time of doing the act or making the omission he is through any disease affecting his mind incapable of understanding what he is doing or of knowing that he ought not do the act or make the omission. (See the penal codes of Kenya, Tanzania and Uganda.)

Machismo: Machismo is the desire of the average male to prove his manliness, a common phenomenon among certain groups and working class males. In some societies it takes the form of knife-fighting, and in others, it is achieved through self-praise, as is common among certain tribes in East Africa such as the Jaluo, the Abakiga, etc. It has been shown that feelings of machismo are aroused by music, films, the presence of women and alcohol. It tends to be characteristic of males in the lower social economic strata, to whom manhood is the most strongly identifying mark. While senior executives and professionals have their positions and property to be proud of, the average worker has nothing to be proud of or to be known for, so his manhood stands out as the greatest criterion of his identity; and to call this into question is to invite trouble.

Mafia: A criminal syndicate that has its origin in Italy and Sicily; it is also known as *Cosa Nostra*, which means "our thing". The organisational structure follows the normal bureaucratic arrangement, with the head being known as the boss and the whole group as a family. Several or many families are organised for the maximisation of operational profit in crime. The binding code of conduct consists of four unbreachable rules:

1. Intense loyalty to the organisation and its ruling elites;
2. Total honesty in relationship with members;
3. The observance of secrecy about the structure, leadership and activities of the organisation; this is *omertà*, the law of silence;
4. Honourable behaviour of members, which they consider to be superior to that of non-members. There is no aspect of human activity in which the Mafia is or may not be involved. Common activities include gambling, horse-racing, prostitution, money laundering, counterfeiting of currency, smuggling, drug trafficking, meddling in politics, restaurant management, transport, and any activity that may be considered profitable (Clinard and Richard 1973).

Magna Carta: The Magna Carta or the Great Charter of 1215 was, as history indicates, one of the earliest bills of human rights. It was drawn up on the orders of John, the king of England, under duress by barons, in 1215. The king was facing mounting opposition almost bordering on national insurrection and the Magna Carta was his response to a widespread outcry from the people who were demanding social, economic and political justice. The Charter guaranteed the privileges of barons and the church against the monarchy and assured jury by trial, though not for commoners. The Magna Carta was the foundation stone of unique English political institutions and the democratic process restricting royal powers and decreed the rights of due process for all freemen, excluding the common people.

The Charter has 63 articles, of which articles 38, 39 and 40 are more explicit on human rights. These state as follows:

38 In future no official shall place a man on trial upon his own unsupported statement, without producing credible witnesses to the truth of it.

39 No free man shall be seized or imprisoned, or stripped of his rights or possessions, or outlawed or exiled, or deprived of his standing in any other way, nor will we proceed with force against him, or send others to do so, except by the lawful judgement of his equals or by the law of the land.

40 To no one will we sell; to no one deny or delay right or justice.

The last paragraph states:

> Given by our hand in the meadow that is called Runnymede between Windsor and Staines, on the fifteenth day of June in the seventeenth year of our reign (Davis, 1971).

Mala fides: Latin for "bad faith".

Malice: An intentional violation of the law to the injury or detriment of another; the wrongful act itself. In libel law, malice usually involves evil intent arising out of hatred or spite.

Malice aforethought: A premeditated intention to do something in order to harm another person; an evil intent arising out of hatred or spite.

Malicious arrest: The arrest of a person on a criminal charge without probable cause, with knowledge that the person did not commit the offence charged.

Malignant anxiety: Malignant anxiety is a mental condition, not quite related to psychosis or mental defect, most commonly found among detribalised people found in cities and towns, who are exposed to serious stress and strains of urban life. It is a common source of capital crime in African slums. This condition was found to be common in Senegal and Kenya and T. Adeoye Lambo, a psychiatrist, found it to be prevalent in Nigeria (Lambo, 1962).

Malpractice: Improper or immoral conduct by a professional in the performance of his or her duties, either intentionally or through carelessness or ignorance. This applies mostly to physicians, surgeons, lawyers, dentists and other public officials.

Matricide: The killing of one's mother; one who kills his or her mother.

Mandamus: In Latin, the word means "we command" and a writ of mandamus is an order issued by higher courts to lower courts or officials directing that something be done or not be done which is within their domain.

Mandatory sentence: A sentence fixed by a legislature for a particular criminal offence. That means that the judge cannot reduce or increase penalty, for example the death penalty is a mandatory or determinate punishment for murder, rape and defilement.

Mania: Two types are medically recognised, with one being a sub-type of the other – the types hypomania and mania.

Hypomania is characterised by a fixed change in the mood of the patient, with the patient being excited and elated. Confidence and optimism and a general feeling of well-being are common. Hypomania is extremely difficult to determine unless one already knows the general demeanour of the patient. In most cases, the patient may be mistaken by the inexperienced to be intoxicated. The behaviour exhibited must be seen to differ from the usual behaviour relative to the patient. Talking becomes excessive and the patient becomes hyperactive in behaviour patterns. While he or she may be very active in speech and activity, the patient is easily distractible; and can change from one activity to another without finishing the task already started. Repetitions and self-elevation are common. In some cases, the excitement and elation may resemble those found in schizophrenics, but the difference is that the hypomaniac can easily establish rapport with his or her observers, who often join in the activity and change as the hypomaniac changes, while in schizophrenia, the elation and excitement of the patient do not attract his or her observers. The hypomaniac is foolhardy; he/she often feels that there is no obstacle too great for him/her to overcome. Hypomaniacs tend to be alert and capable of noticing many things, and it is often due to this factor that they are so distractible both in speech and action. They tend to be extremely childish but very friendly, always attempting to manage the affairs of others and in this way they are very often a nuisance to others. They have no idea of their condition since they feel elated and very fit. Any effort that may appear to thwart or frustrate a maniac or a hypomaniac may generate not only anger and resentment but also violence. Linford Rees gives very interesting illustrations of this condition; one of which is as follows:

> A male patient is about 56 with an attack of hypomania; he gets up early in the morning with a great deal of energy, is very active, singing in the bath, talking, a great deal of slapping people on the back, making jokes and puns. He may start decorating his house, e.g. he may start painting the front door and before finishing he will start dismantling his car and then start digging the garden, at the same time talking with rapidity to anyone nearby, giving advice and often interfering with their affairs. He feels very fit, wants to be doing everything at once and is readily distracted by external stimuli. He will tend to go off buying things, things that he does not need or cannot afford; he may change his car unnecessarily or buy new outfits of clothes. He is excessively generous; giving away money by cheque that cannot be met. If anybody thwarts him he will get angry, even violent. He may go off to the local pub and drink excessively, buying everyone drinks, incessantly talking and making puns. He makes rash promises to do things for people and feels that nothing is impossible for him to achieve. Such a state of over-activity and drive continues through the day and until the early morning, as he regards going to sleep as a waste of time (Linford-Rees, 1967).

Mannheim, Hermann (1889): Born in Germany, studied law; became a judge of the court of appeal in Berlin and later a professor of law at the University of Berlin. He later taught law and criminology at London School of Economics and Political Science of the University of London. Became president of the senate of the Court of Appeal in West Germany. His writings include *The Dilemma of Penal Reform* (1939), *War and Crime* (1941) and *Comparative Criminology* in two volumes (1965).

Manslaughter: A homicide that is neither lawful nor accidental but not amounting to the crime of murder. Manslaughter may be committed in a number of ways; if the original charge of murder is reduced to manslaughter owing to apparent lack of *mens rea*, or if the defendant was suffering from diminished responsibility, or if the homicide was committed while under the influence of alcohol or as a result of a suicide pact. The penalty for manslaughter is life imprisonment.

Marginal man: This is a person with a dilemma, or in a state of mental conflict, by reason of his/her participation in two but distinct cultural groups. Such a person is not fully loyal and committed to the values and standards of either group, nor fully accepted by any of the two groups. All this is due to inadequate socialisation and failure on the part of the individual concerned to internalise one or both cultures adequately. The nearest concept is detribalisation, common in urban settings where such marginal persons are found.

Marijuana: The dried leaves, flowering tops and stems of hemp, used as an intoxicating or hallucinogenic drug, usually smoked in cigarettes; *Cannabis sativa*.

Marx, Karl: (1818 – 1883) Marx was the founder of scientific communism, historical and dialectical materialism, and scientific political economy, the leader and teacher of the World Proletariat. Born in Trier in the Rhineland, Prussia, his family was Jewish but converted to Christianity soon after the Napoleonic war in order to avoid persecution. He studied law at the University of Bonn and the University of Berlin; soon he turned to study philosophy and his thesis was on "The Difference Between the Natural Philosophies of Democratus and Epicurus". Submitted to the University of Jena, it earned him a degree of Doctor of Philosophy. In the thesis Marx compared the theories of Democratus, which stressed determinism and those of Epicurus, which focused on the freedom of man's consciousness to change his environment.

He taught at the University of Bonn but soon became involved in journalism and wrote for and later edited the *Rheineische Zeitung*. In a short period of time he had made a strong impression on his contemporaries, with one of these, Moses Hess, writing to a friend:

> The greatest, perhaps the only, genuine philosopher now alive, who will soon attract the eyes of all Germany, Dr Marx will give medieval religion and politics their *coup de grâce*. He combines the deepest philosophical seriousness with the most biting wit. Imagine Rousseau, Voltaire, Holbach, Lessing, Heine and Hegel, fused into one person – fused, not juxtaposed – and you have Dr Marx.

Because of his radical views, Marx had to move from Bonn to Paris, and later to London. In 1848, together with a fellow German, Frederick Engels, he published *The Communist Manifesto*; Marx later published *Das Capital*. He died in London in 1883 (McLellan, 1980).

Masturbation: This is sexual stimulation usually by oneself; it is achieved by manipulating the sexual organs in order to bring about sexual orgasm; in some communities it is regarded as deviant behaviour.

Mayhem: This is defined as violent deprivation of another person of such of his members as may render him or her less able to fight in self-defence or to fight the enemy. These injuries include cutting off of hands or feet, or plucking out of eyes, making the victim incapable of defending himself; dismemberment.

Mediation: A process whereby an independent person, not necessarily a lawyer, arranges to reconcile spouses or any group of people involved in dispute without having to resort to a court of law. One of the social mechanisms of resolving social conflicts.

Mens legis: Latin for "the mind of the law"; it means the purpose, the spirit or the intention of a law.

Mens rea: The concept of *mens rea* is very often used in a broad sense to mean evil intent or knowledge of the wrongfulness of behaviour, but the accuser's ignorance of the law or the moral wrongness of the behaviour is generally no defence, although a reasonable belief in the existence of facts which would render his conduct innocent is usually a defence. Very often the expression *mens rea* is used in the Latin maxim *actus non facit reum, nisi mens sit rea*; that is, an act does not make a person guilty unless his mind is guilty. Other concepts used instead of *mens rea* are: malice aforethought, evil intent, recklessness, guilty conscience, and guilty knowledge. The concept of *mens rea* should not be confused with motive. Motive is understood to mean the moral nature or quality of intent; it is the moving force. Motive is the ulterior intent, the ulterior design, the personal end sought to be accomplished by an act other than the immediate consequences of the act. For example, two men may be competing for the love of one girl; one of the men may plan to kill the other; and if he succeeds, the planning to kill is the *mens rea*, while the desire to be the only lover of the woman is the motive.

Mental handicap: Impairment of intelligence, which can range from mild to severe. In the more severe cases it is associated with social problems and difficulty in living independently. Individuals may be born with mental handicaps, but others may develop it as a result of brain damage or illness.

Mental retardation: A state of arrested development of the mind existing from birth or from an early age. Mental retardation is also called amentia, mental deficiency, or mental sub-normality; it varies in severity and results from a variety of causes. Three types are identified:

1) The slightly retarded, with an intelligence quotient (IQ) of 50 to 70;
2) The moderately retarded, with an IQ of 30 to 50;
3) The severely retarded, with an IQ of below 30(Linford-Rees, 1967).

Mischief: Malicious damage to another's property.

Misdemeanour: A lesser offence than a felony, for example simple theft, such as stealing a pumpkin from a garden. The punishment for misdemeanour is either a fine, a short prison sentence or probation with or without supervision.

Misdirection: An incorrect direction by a judge to a jury on a matter of the law. In such cases, the court of appeal may quash the conviction.

Misprision: Failure to report a crime. A person commits the crime of misprision if he or she knows or reasonably suspects that someone has committed treason but does not report this fact to the relevant authorities within a reasonable time.

Mitigation: The reduction in the severity of the penalty being awarded to an offender. Before a sentence is passed on a convicted offender, the defence may make a plea in mitigation, putting forward reasons for making the sentence less severe than it would otherwise be. These reasons may include the personal character of the offender, the time he or she has spent on remand, being a first offender, penalty obligations etc.

Modernisation: A social, economic and political process by which individuals, groups or communities undergo change in their traditional values, attitudes and psychological orientations while adapting to the impact of urbanisation, and industrialisation as a result of social change. This process, directly or indirectly, provides a conducive social milieu for deviance and criminality (Huntington, 1970).

Molestation: This refers to behaviour that has the effect or intention of annoying or pestering one's spouse or children.

Molestation need not involve an act of violence or physical assault, and in this respect, harassment may constitute molestation.

Money laundering: A process involving financial transactions intended to conceal the ultimate source of money holdings. The process is used widely to camouflage illegal activities, which may include drug trafficking, corruption, fraud, money earned from organised prostitution and tax evasion.

Monism: A theory that national and international laws form part of one legal structure, in which the international law is supreme. The opposite of this view is dualism, which holds that national and international laws constitute two separate legal structures, which operate in different fields.

Moot: A term used to describe a controversy that has ended or evolved to the stage where a court decision on that particular cause is no longer relevant or even necessary; this places a limitation on the process of the courts to decide on the case.

Moral punishment: Proposed by Van Bemmeleu, moral punishment consists of graded stages:

(1) Reprimand
(2) Severe reprimand
(3) Censure
(4) Severe censure
(5) Serious censure with reminder

A reminder, when issued by a court, would amount to a mandatory prison sentence when further crime is committed (Bemmeleu, 1968).

Mores: The manners and ways of a social group, that have become acceptable behaviour and have become essential to the group's welfare and survival but have not become part of the group's criminal law.

Mortgage: A loan using a real asset such as a house, a building or a piece of land as collateral. If the interest or the redemption payments are not paid, the lender or mortgagee can foreclose on the collateral, that is, he or she can take over and sell it to repay the loan. Mortgages have a life span ranging from some months to several or many years, depending on the terms of the mortgage agreed upon.

Motive: The purpose behind an action. Motive is not, under normal conditions, relevant in the decision of guilt or innocence. For example, killing someone in order to save him or her from more suffering is either murder or manslaughter. In the same way, a bad motive is not relevant in deciding legal guilt; a good motive may be considered as a mitigating fact in deciding the penalty in convictions.

Murder: This is one type of criminal homicide. Murder is an unlawful killing of a human being by another with malice aforethought or *mens rea*, which denotes a guilty mind. Murder, in east Africa, is a capital offence, which carries a mandatory death penalty. Malice aforethought is believed to be established if it can be shown that:

(a) there was intention to cause death or grievous bodily harm to a person. This is outright and overt malice.

(b) there existed the knowledge that the act or the omission will cause death or grievous harm to the person; in this case malice is implied.

(c) there was an intent to commit a felony, as in the use of violence or road robbery.

(d) there was an intention to facilitate the escape of a felon from custody in order to avoid arrest and persecution (Mushanga, 1974a).

Mutilation: A form of penalty in which the victim's hands and feet are cut off and his eyes plucked out. This kind of treatment is justified "because it prevents the repetition of a particular crime". This form of mutilation is also known as dismemberment.

N

Narcotic: A substance used to induce drowsiness, sleep, stupor or insensibility; used over a period of time it affects the mind negatively.

Natural law: The permanent underlying basis of all law; a kind of perfect or ideal justice given to man by nature to which man's law should conform as closely as possible. Natural law is distinguished from positive law, which is a body of laws imposed on a society by the state.

Natural rights: The fundamental rights to which all human beings are entitled without the interference of the state. The basis of this is that all human beings are by nature free and equal and have inherent natural rights that must be passed on from generation to generation.

NB (nota bene): Latin for "note well".

Necessitas non habet legem: Latin which means "necessity has no law".

Necessity: Pressure of circumstances that may compel an otherwise law-abiding citizen to commit a criminal act. For example, a starving person, that is a person who has not had food or water for several days, may steal food in order to ward off imminent death due to starvation.

Negligence: Failure to exercise a degree of care that a person of ordinary prudence or a reasonable man would exercise under similar circumstances.

Nemo est supra legis: Latin which means "nobody is above the law".

Neurosis: A general term denoting emotional disorders such as anxiety, obsession and depression. The common characteristic is mood, but unlike in psychosis contact with reality is generally unaffected.

Nihil: Latin for "nothing", or "not at all", commonly abbreviated as "nil".

Nolle prosequi: Latin meaning "not willing to prosecute", it is a legal decision taken by the Director of Public Prosecution not to proceed with prosecution in a criminal case. A criminal case in which a *nolle proseque* has been entered is not the same as an acquittal; a further prosecution can always be instituted.

Nolo contendere: Latin meaning "I will not contest it". In law, it is equivalent to a guilty plea.

Nominal: Means " in name only"; inconsiderable or trivial.

Nominee: One who has been asked to act for another in a particular context, such as a trustee or an agent; a person who has been nominated as a candidate for an office.

Non compos mentis: Latin for "not of sound mind".

Norms: These are informal guidelines about what is or is not considered normal social behaviour, as opposed to laws and rules, which are formal guidelines. These shared norms vary from one society to another and even from one situation to another and range from crucial taboos such as incest, bestiality or cannibalism to trivial customs such as the correct way of greeting elders. Norms form part of a group's culture and are an important element of social control.

Nugatory: Void, invalid; for example, judicial proceedings in courts that lack jurisdiction.

Nuisance: A wrong arising out of unreasonable or unlawful use of property, to the annoyance or damage of another or of the public.

O

Od. (omni die): Latin for "every day".

Oath: A pronouncement swearing the truth of a statement or promise, usually by an appeal to God to witness its truth. An oath is required for various purposes, particularly for affidavits and for giving evidence in courts. The usual oath given in court is as:

> I swear by the Almighty God, that the evidence which I shall give shall be the truth, the whole truth and nothing but the truth.

Those who object to taking an oath on the grounds of their religion or because they profess no religion are usually required to affirm rather than take the oath.

Obiter dicta: Latin for "passing or incidental statements". Statements made or decisions reached in a court's opinion that were not necessary to disposition of the case.

Obscene: Offensive to the senses or to the mind, lewd, repulsive or indecent.

Obsolescence: A process by which property becomes useless, not because of physical deterioration, but because of scientific or technological advances.

Obstruction of justice: Impeding those who seek justice in a court, or of those who have duties or powers of administering justice therein, including attempting to influence, intimidate or impede any juror, witness or officer in any court regarding the discharge of his or her duties.

Occupational crime: A term used to refer to a wide range of crimes committed by persons in the course of their occupations; when the offences are committed by the entire firm, association or industry, such crimes are referred to as organisational crimes or corporate crime (Clinard and Meier, 1992).

Occupational hazard: A risk distinctively associated with a particular type of employment or workplace.

Oedipus complex: According to Freud, the Greek word Oedipus refers to the complex of emotions aroused in the young child by a subconscious sexual desire for the parent of the opposite sex and a wish to exclude the parent of the same sex. In this complex, a male child has sexual desire for the mother and desires the elimination of the father.

Of counsel: Refers to an attorney who assists in the preparation of a case, but who is not the principal attorney of record for the case.

Offence: A crime. The common term for crimes is offences. Offences are classified into indictable, and also as arrestable and non-arrestable.

Offences against the person: Crimes that involve the use or threat of physical force against another person. The common offences against the person include homicide, infanticide, rape, assault, aggravated assault, battery, abortion, causing death by careless driving, torture, wounding, causing or inflicting grievous bodily harm, kidnapping and all crimes of indecency.

Omission: Neglect or failure to perform some act required by law or private obligation.

Op. cit. (opere citato): Latin for "in the work cited".

Order maintenance: Order is defined as the absence of disorder, which means, in turn, behaviour that tends to disrupt the peace and tranquility of the public or that involves face-to-face conflict of two or more persons.

Outlaw: A fugitive from the law; a person who is deprived of the protection of the law.

Ovem lupo committere: Latin for "to entrust the sheep to the wolf".

Overrule: To overturn or make void the holding or decision of a prior case, generally accomplished in a different and subsequent case; when a court renders a subsequent decision that is opposite to the decision made by a prior court.

Overt act: Open act, especially an outward act done in furtherance of a crime and a manifestation of an intent to accomplish the crime.

Ownership: Exclusive right of possessing, enjoying and disposing of a thing.

P

Pactum: Latin for "pact"; contract or agreement.

Paedophile: A person who is sexually attracted to children of either sex.

Pander: To pimp; to cater for the lust of another. A pander is a pimp, a procurer, a male bawd. Pandering is the crime of inducing a female to become a prostitute.

Paralegal: A person who is not a licensed attorney but has some legal skills and can work under the supervision of an attorney. Some of the paralegal persons in Uganda are employed as lay magistrates and court brokers, etc.

Paramour: One's lover; one in the place of a husband or wife, but without the legal rights attached to the marital relationship.

Paraphilias: *Para* from the Greek meaning "to the side of" and *philios* meaning "loving". Paraphilias are bizarre or abnormal sexually deviant practices which involve recurrent sexual urges focused on non-human objects of any description; receiving or giving pain through a sexual activity, or subjecting children to such activity when they are not able to give their consent.

Parole: A process whereby an offender is released from prison before he or she completes his or her prison sentence and is supervised by a parole officer in the community. There are usually conditions to be observed, the non-observance of which will lead to the parole being revoked and the offender returned to prison to complete his or her sentence.

Parricide: The killing of a very close relative.

Parties: Persons who are involved together in some transaction, e.g. people who are involved in a deed or contract. Also people who are involved in litigation, either civil or criminal.

Patent: Evident, obvious.

Patent infringement: The act of trespassing upon the rights secured by a patent.

Paternity suit: A suit initiated to determine the paternity of a child born out of wedlock and to provide for the support of that child once the paternity has been established.

Patricide: The criminal act of one killing his or her own father.

Pawn: To deposit personal property with another as security for the payment of a debt.

Peaceful coexistence: A principle of relations between states with diametrically opposed social systems (e.g. socialism and capitalism) that implies renunciation of armed conflict or war as a means of settling controversial issues.

Peculation: The fraudulent misappropriation to one's own; use of money or goods entrusted to one's care.

Pecuniary: That which consists of money or that which can be valued in money. A pecuniary loss is a loss of money or a loss that can be translated into economic loss.

Pederasty: Sodomy; anal intercourse between males, especially between an adult male and a young person.

Peine de mort, peine perdue: French for "death penalty is useless penalty".

Penitentiary: Originally an institution intended to keep offenders in isolation from one another in order that they have time to reflect on their bad conduct and become penitent. This term is synonymous with prison.

Per capita: Latin for "by the heads"; anything referred to as per capita means that it is calculated by the number of persons or heads involved and is divided equally among all. For example, the per capita income of Uganda is the amount of money each individual Ugandan would receive if the whole income of Uganda were divided among all Ugandans equally. The per capita of Uganda in 2005 was reported to be $1,400, compared to USA's $ 38,800 (*The World Almanac,* 2005).

Per curiam: Latin for "by the court", which refers to action or a decision by the whole court or by the Chief Justice on behalf of the court other than by a single judge.

Persona non grata: Used in international diplomacy to denote a diplomat who is not acceptable to a foreign government. In Latin it means "unacceptable person", and is commonly abbreviated as p.n.g.

Personality: In psychology, personality refers to the sum total of a person's psychological and physical characteristics which make him or her a unique person. The term includes his or her behavioural tendencies, his or her intellectual qualities and his or her emotional disposition. Psychologists have conclusively determined that:-

> Every person is in certain respects
> Like all other people,
> Like some other people,
> Like no other person.
> (Pervin, 1984).

Perverse verdict: A decision by a jury that goes against the established law as stated by the presiding judge.

Petition: A complaint or prayer to the court or judge seeking justice in respect of something someone feels is wrong. It is commonly presented in written form, stating facts and circumstances relied upon as a cause for judicial action.

Pickpocket: A person who steals from the pockets of others, a thief.

Pilferage: Theft, especially of small quantities of very little value; also known as shoplifting.

Plagiarism: Appropriation of the literary composition, the product of the mind and language of another, and passing

140

it off as one's own. In law, this is known as infringement of copyright and it is a crime.

Plain view: A doctrine that may legitimise a search or seizure without a search warrant, which is otherwise generally required.

Plaintiff: In a civil case, one who brings the complaint against the defendant, a complainant in civil proceedings; one harmed by the defendant.

Plea: An answer to an accusation or charge before a judical officer or tribunal.

Plea bargain: An agreement between the prosecution and defence in which the defendant agrees to plead guilty instead of not guilty in return for the reduced charge or when the court makes it apparent that the sentence will be considerably less severe if the defendant pleaded guilty.

Police: A governmental department (of state, city or town) for maintaining law and order and for detecting offenders; its main objective is preventing and controlling crime.

The police as an occupation is heavily tainted. The origin of this stigma is unknown but has its roots in history. In medieval times watchmen, who later became policemen, were recruited from among the ranks of the destitute and the uneducated.

Later, these watchmen were used by kings and dictators in underground aspects of tyranny and political repression and were both despised and feared. At present the police is regarded by the majority with distrust and fear, especially in East Africa. They are despised by others because of the low requirements for entry and feared by many because of the force the police sometimes applies in dealing with law violators. It is generally held that one of the primary roles of the police is to prevent crime. But close examination of the routine duties of police officers reveals very little, if any, evidence that they undertake activities that may be related to the prevention of crime. Generally, their role is to detect, arrest and prosecute offenders; and none of these activities is preventive in the sense of obviating criminality. It is possible that the police, by holding, arresting and generally harrassing civilians may actually contribute to lawlessness and refusal by the public to report crimes.

Political crime: A criminal act is referred to as political when its perpetrator has the intention to influence or change the political agenda within the country. The criminal act may be completely indistinguishable from any other traditional criminal act; it could be a homicide of an incumbent president as when president John F. Kennedy of the United States was assassinated; it could be a kidnapping of a presidential or parliamentary candidate, or an assault on a political opponent (Haskell and Yablonsky, 1974).

Populus vult decipi, ergo decipiatur: Latin meaning "the public wishes to be fooled, therefore let it be fooled".

Pornography: The word 'pornography' is derived from the Greek in which *orne* means prostitute and *graphein* means to write. It is now common to find, in many cities, stores devoted to the display and sale of books, magazines and films that depict explicit sexual acts of every kind. The purpose of this is to provide sexual relief and excitement for paying customers.

Positive school: The positive school of criminology is also known as the "scientific school" or the "Italian school" after the work of Lombrosa (1836–1906). This school of thought marked the beginning of the study of crime causation, of emphasis on the nature of the criminal person rather than on the nature of the criminal act per se (Vold, 1970).

Positivism: A branch of social sciences that uses the scientific method of the natural sciences to suggest that human behaviour is a product of social, biological, economic and psychological forces.

Pot: Slang for marijuana.

Poverty: A social as well as an economic condition in which an individual, family or a social group lacks the resources necessary for subsistence. Poverty is the greatest enemy of democracy, the rule of law and happiness; it destroys liberty, freedom and independence, makes the observance of moral values and virtues impracticable, and retards social progress. In the Third World countries of Africa and Asia, poverty is said to be the cause of soaring crime rates and delinquency. In this regard, fighting poverty and social inequality is one of the ways to fight crime and delinquency (Clinard and Abbott, 1973; O'Connor,1991).

Power: "Power tends to corrupt, absolute power corrupts absolutely" – attributed to Lord Acton (1838–1902); the ability to do or act; ability to influence others to do what one wishes.

Precedent: Previously decided cases recognised as authority for the disposition of cases.

Prescription: An assumption of fact resulting from a rule of law that requires such fact to be assured from another fact or a set of facts.

Presumption of innocence: A prevailing assumption that the accused person remains innocent until proved guilty. Because of this assumption the government is under a legal obligation to prove the guilt of the accused beyond reasonable doubt.

Presumptive evidence: Evidence that is indirect or circumstantial; prima facie evidence or evidence that is not conclusive and admits explanation or contradiction.

Preventive patrol: Police officers are not dispatched to crime spots or to conduct routine law and order maintenance, they merely walk or drive around in their areas of operation without necessarily looking for troublemakers. This kind of work is referred to as preventive patrol in that the mere presence of the police in the area will deter people from engaging in criminal activity.

Prima facie: From Latin, meaning "first appearance"; at first appearance, or on the face of things.

Privacy: A general right to be left alone, and not be interfered with by the state or by members of the public unjustifiably.

Privity: A relationship between parties out of which arises mutuality of interest.

Privy: A person connected with another or having mutual interests with him or her in the same action; a thing, by contract or otherwise.

Probable cause: A requisite element of valid arrest or search and seizure; it consists of knowledge of facts and circumstances sufficient in themselves to warrant the belief that a crime has been committed or that property subject to seizure is at a designated location.

Probation: A judicial decision to permit a convicted person to go free under supervision by a probation officer in the hope that he or she will live a law-abiding life thereafter. During the probationary period, he or she must obey certain conditions set out by the court in the probation order or else he or she will be returned to prison.

Procedure of trial: Criminal cases in East Africa are heard by judicial officers, that is the magistrates (both lay and lawyers) and the judges. More serious crimes such as murder, treason, and rape are usually tried by High Court judges, but the preliminary inquiries are normally conducted by magistrates. The following is the schedule of the sequence of a trial:

1. After the arrest (sooner or later) the suspect is brought before the court for formal charge. After the charge has been read to the defendant or suspect, he or she may elect to reply by either (a) denying the charge (not guilty) or (b) by accepting the charge (the plea of guilty).

2. The opening statement of the case by the prosecution.
3. The opening statement of the defence.
4. Presentation of the evidence by the prosecution and proof of the crime charged.
5. Direct examination by the prosecution of its witnesses.
6. Cross-examination by the defence of the prosecution witnesses.
7. The defence may then present its evidence of negative or raising doubt as to the evidence presented by the prosecution.
8. The defence may follow by direct examination of its witnesses.
9. The court may allow the prosecution to re-open its case.
10. The prosecution may then cross-examine the defence witnesses.
11. The defence may make a closing argument, followed by the prosecution's argument, unless the case ends without counteracting arguments.
12. In a jury system (where there are assessors) the court may instruct the assessors about their duty and the law relating to the subject matter and how it is to be applied in regard to facts and evidence presented.
13. In a court where there is a jury or assessors, they return their verdict.
14. Finally, the judge reads his or her judgement in a language which both parties understand.

Professional criminal: A professional criminal is one whose life revolves around theft, who is skilled in the ways of criminality, and who views him/herself as a professional criminal, abiding by a set of rules and values.

Prostitution: Possibly the second oldest profession, the first being midwifery, is defined as the bartering of sexual favours for monetary consideration, either as cash or gifts, without any emotional attachment between partners. Prostitution must be differentiated from sexual promiscuity, which is a widely practised sexual behaviour but not directly related to monetary considerations. Prostitution and related illegal conduct, such as soliciting, managing a brothel etc. are crimes in Uganda.

Prudence: Precaution, attentiveness, good judgement; a degree of care required by law in certain dealings with other people.

Psychiatrist: A physician who has been trained and has experience in the diagnosis and treatment of psychiatric illness.

Psychiatry: Psychiatry is the branch of medicine which deals with the diagnosis, treatment and prevention of mental abnormalities and disorders. It deals with illnesses which affect a person's mental behaviour, i.e. his feelings, thinking, and his social relationships.

There are four main branches of psychiatry:
1. Child psychiatry deals with psychiatric problems of children.
2. Psychogeriatrics is psychiatry of old age.
3. Forensic psychiatry deals with medico-legal aspects of psychiatry.
4. Social psychiatry deals with all problems of human ecology and epidemiology.
Psychiatry has been defined as the only medical specialty that does not focus on a single part of the human body.

Psychologist: A person who has specialised training in the structure and function of the human mind, but is not concerned with mental illness.

Psychopath: In most legal systems, psychopathy is not classified as an illness; it merely implies diminished responsibility rather than full exculpation. Psychopaths include people exhibiting temporary mental disturbance, feeblemindedness and other pathological mental conditions. Psychiatrists' definition of a psychopath is that he or she lacks social responsibility and general consideration for others. The psychopath is characterised by an antisocial mode of conduct, which ranges from inefficiency and lack of interest in any form of occupation to pathological lying, swindling, alcoholism, drug addiction, sexual offences and violence with little or no self-control. Also known as **sociopath.**

Strictly speaking, the term does not refer to any intellectual defect, psychosis, neurosis, or even schizophrenia, but only to the antisocial and delinquent.

The psychopath can be identified by his immaturity, self-centredness, having little or no regard for the rights or convenience of others, the desire for immediate, almost spontaneous, gratification of his or her frequent and uninhibited desires, and quick resort to the use of violence, frustration and lack of conscience or sense of guilt.

Psychopathic disorders are disorders of personality, whether there is subnormal intelligence or not. The sociological definition of a psychopath is a person who, from an early age, shows abnormality of behaviour of an antisocial nature with a tendency to act on impulse to satisfy the immediate desires without reference to the consequences of his or her actions. Studies have shown that personality traits are, to some extent, determined by heredity but that the environment may largely control the expression of the personality disposition.

Psychopaths can be extremely dangerous because of their disregard for other people's welfare; and these behaviours lead to violence and forcible rapes.

Psychosomatic: This term refers to the influence of psychological factors in the production and manifestation of physical disorders.

Public hostility towards the police: In the majority of nations, the police are held in low esteem and the public nurse considerable hostility towards them. The police are held to be corrupt, and are often suspected to facilitate criminal gangs and to shield wealthy political crooks. As a result of these perceptions, the police are generally not accorded high social status.

Public mischief: A person who deliberately misleads a police officer to carry out an investigation by accusing another person of having committed an offence, usually to divert attention from him/herself.

Public nuisance: Behaviour that unreasonably interferes with the health, safety, peace, comfort or convenience of the community.

Punishment: The practice of imposing something unpleasant or aversive on a person in response to unwanted, disobedient or morally wrong behaviour.

Punitive damages: Extra damages awarded to a plaintiff in a civil lawsuit because of the special character of the wrong done, or to punish and make an example of the defendant in order to deter others.

Q

Quash: To invalidate a conviction by an inferior court or to set aside a decision subject to judicial review.

Qui facit per alium facit per se: Latin for "he who acts through another is himself responsible".

Quid pro quo: Latin for "something for something". Sometimes used as synonymous with consideration, sometimes referred to as quid, indicating that which a party receives or is promised.

Quittance: An act of releasing someone from a legal obligation.

R

Race: In anthropology a race is a human population that is sufficiently inbred to reveal a distinctive genetic composition manifest in a distinctive combination of physical traits (Hoebel, 1966).

Racketeer: One who lives by crime; a member of a gang of lawbreakers and especially one who blackmails by intimidation.

Radzinowicz: Sir Leon, LLD (Geneva), LLD (Cracow) LLD (Rome), LLD (Cambridge), Honorary LLD (Leicester); for long professor Radzinowicz was professor of criminology and director of the Institute of Criminology at the University of Cambridge. He was chairman of the Scientific Committee of the Council of Europe. His main contribution was his four monumental volumes of *The History of English Criminal Law* (1948 –1968) and *Ideology and Crime* (1966).

Ransom: Money or any other consideration paid for the release of a kidnapped or otherwise captured person or thing; to redeem a person or a thing by payment in cash or in kind.

Rape: This is sexual intercourse, anal or vaginal, with a woman or another man without their consent, as a result of the use of force or threats, or because the victim was asleep or unconscious, or very drunk or consent was obtained through fraud. It is also rape with a person who is mentally deranged in such a way that she or he is not capable of understanding what is being consented to. In Uganda the punishment for rape is death.

Rapine: An act in which one person with force openly takes the personal property of another.

Ratification: Sanctioning or affirming confirmation of the act of another regardless of whether the act was originally authorised. The process by which a society approves a fundamental change in the law.

Ratify: To confirm; to approve; to legalise an act.

Ratio legis: Latin for "legal reasoning" or grounds; the underlying principles; theory, doctrine or science of the law.

Ravish: Generally synonymous with rape. Literally, to ravish is to seize or to snatch by force.

Re: Latin for "in the matter of"; in law it means "in the case of..."

Real evidence: This is evidence in the form of material objects such as weapons or tools used in the commission of a crime.

Real property: Land and whatever is erected or growing on it, or affixed to it.

Realisation: This refers to the conversion of an asset into money.

Reasonable man: In law the reasonable man is the ordinary citizen, who in England is referred to as the "man on the Clapham omnibus". The standard of care in actions for negligence is based on what a reasonable person might be expected to do.

Rebut: To refute or oppose; to put forward evidence that denies the truth of the accusation.

Rebuttal evidence: Any evidence that refutes, counteracts or explains away evidence given by a witness or an adverse party.

Recaption: The retaking of goods that have been taken wrongfully or have been withheld wrongfully.

Receiver: A neutral person appointed by a court to receive and preserve the property that is the subject of litigation during the period of litigation; or to manage and dispose of the property as the court may direct.

Recidivism: This is a condition in which a person charged, convicted and sentenced repeats the same offence or any other offence. The probability of repeating a criminal offence varies with the age of the offender. It is generally recognised that the younger the person is at the time of committing an offence for the first time, the higher the probability that he or she will commit a second offence and the shorter the interval between the first and second offences (Sellin, 1958).

Reciprocity: Generally, a relationship between persons, corporations, states or countries whereby privileges granted by one are returned by another. A very central element in diplomacy.

Recognition: In international law, recognition is a process by which a state declares that another political entity fulfils the conditions of statehood and as a result of this it is willing to deal with the new entity as a full member of the international community. In common practice, such recognition is followed by exchange of diplomats and setting up diplomatic missions.

Recognisance: An agreement entered into before a magistrate by which an accused person is released "on his or her own recognisance" without bail, on his or her undertaking to keep the peace or obey any other court instruction.

Recovery: The establishment of a right by the judgement of a court, though it does not imply return to whole or normal.

Recusal: A legal requirement whereby a judge or attorney offers to withdraw from a case before the court because of conflict of interest.

Red-handed: Someone is said to have been caught red-handed if he or she is caught physically committing the crime. Lule is said to have been found red-handed when he is caught cutting down a bunch of bananas from Musoke's banana garden.

Reductio ad absurdum: Latin for "to reduce to the absurd"; to disprove a legal argument by showing that it ultimately leads to an absurd position.

Referendum: Referring legislative acts to the voters for final approval or rejection.

Reformation: In penology, reformation is deemed to be one of the aims of penal sanction under which an offender gives up his or her criminal behaviour and becomes a law-abiding citizen.

Refugee: A refugee is a person who flees his or her native country and seeks shelter and security in a foreign country. Reasons for people seeking refuge range from persons or groups fleeing from persecution by the state or by another dominant group, or from war, natural disasters or pandemic diseases.

Relicit: A survivor of a married couple that is either a widow or a widower.

Reparation: In law, reparation must, as far as possible, wipe out all the consequences of the illegal act committed by one group of people against others, or a nation or nations against another or others so as to re-establish the situation which would, in all probability, have existed if that act had not been committed (Shaw, 1997).

Repeal: The cancelling of a previous law; to revoke or rescind; to withdraw any resolution or privilege.

Res: Latin meaning "a thing"; in law it refers to any object or subject matter that is the basis of a civil action.

Respondent: The party called upon to answer in any legal proceeding; also known as a defendant.

Restitution: The punishment that requires the offender to repay the victim with services or money. This punishment may be instead of or in addition to other punishment or fine. It can also be a requirement of parole.

Retainer: The hiring of a lawyer or any other professional counsellor; also the fee such an official will be paid by the client.

Retraction: The withdrawal of a plea, declaration, accusation, promise, etc.

Retreatism: A form of deviant behaviour in which the individual rejects the culturally defined goals of success and the institutionalised means of attaining them. Retreatism is a mode of adaptation to the frustration of being unable to attain culturally valued goals. Drug addiction, alcoholism and some kinds of hobbies are some of the common traits of retreatists.

Retroactive: Refers to a rule of law, whether administrative or judicial, that relates to things decided in the past.

Retroactive law: A law that relates back to a previous transaction and gives it some different legal effect from that which it had under the law when it occurred.

Retrograde amnesia: A mental condition in which a person loses his/her memory of events and experiences which occurred prior to an illness, accident, injury or traumatic experience such as rape or an accident. The amnesia may cover a longer or shorter period of time and usually declines over time when earlier memories begin to return before the most recent ones.

Reversal: As used in opinions and judgements, the vacating or changing to the contrary the decisions of a lower court or other body.

Reversible error: An error which affects substantially an applicant's legal rights and obligations that, if uncorrected, would result in a miscarriage of justice, which justifies the reversal of the judgement of the inferior court.

Review: A reconsideration or re-examination by the same court or body of its former decision; or the re-examination by an appellate court of the record of the lower court's determination that is an appeal to an appellate court.

Revocation: Recall of authority conferred; cancellation of an offer by the offeror which, if effective, terminates the offeree's power of acceptance.

Rigor mortis: Latin for "stiffness of death". A medical term referring to the stiffness of a body that occurs some hours after death, which normally disappears when decomposition of the body sets in.

Right: Individual liberties as outlined in a national constitution, for example, the right to life, to privacy or to run for office or to be voted to office.

Royalty: A share of the product or the proceeds therefrom, received by an owner for permitting another to exploit and use his property. The term is usually used for mining leases, literary works, inventions and other intellectual productions.

Rule of law: The supremacy of law; this implies that nobody is above the law unless the basic law, i.e. the constitution, stipulates so. The rule of law as a legal ideal is for the regulation of relations among men. This doctrine is derived from the work of Dicey, who outlines three major elements:

1. *The absence of arbitrary power.* On this Dicey (1885) states "... no man is punishable or can be lawfully made to suffer in body or goods except for a distinct breach of law established in the ordinary legal manner before the ordinary courts of the land"; in this regard, the rule of law is contracted with the system of governments that are based on the exercises of people in authority with wide unlimited power.

2. *The subjection of officials to the ordinary courts* so that the courts can press judgement between officials and citizens. This means that "...no man is above the law"and that "...every man whatever his rank or condition, is subject to the ordinary law of the realm and amenable to the jurisdiction of the ordinary tribunal."

3. *The constitution: The result of the ordinary law of the land.* Dicey states that "...the general principles of the constitution (for example the right to personal liberty, or the right of public meeting) are with us as a result

of judicial decisions determining the right of private persons in particular cases brought before the courts". In this respect, the rule of law requires that the people be subjected to the law of the land (laws made by men) and not of men, "for when men rule, despotism, corruption, tyranny and brutality rein, laws become the means of oppressing the ruled" (Dicey, 1885).

S

Sadism: A psychological orientation in which an individual derives pleasure from inflicting pain and suffering on a victim, especially in a sexual relationship.

Sadomasochism: Deriving sexual pleasure from receiving pain from or inflicting it on another person.

Sanction: A sanction may be positive or negative. It is a social reaction to a mode of individual or group behaviour. In the positive sense, a sanction is a reward, while it becomes a penalty when it is negative. A negative sanction is intended to discourage the disapproved behaviour while a positive sanction, such as a promotion, is intended to encourage the approved behaviour. Positive sanctions include promotions, applause, praise, gifts, medals and certificates. Negative sanctions include ridicule, disapproval, demotion, imprisonment, fines; the death penalty by firing squad is an extreme example.

Social sanctions function in a cultural milieu, where they may be incorporated as aspects of social control. A look of disapproval may restrain an individual from a certain mode of behaviour if he or she is a member of the cultural group and has come to understand the meaning attached to such a glance.

Scapegoating: This is placing the blame for one's trouble, failures, frustrations or sense of guilt on some other innocent person or group. The term is derived from the Hebrew ancient practice, when, once a year, they symbolically placed all their sins on a goat and then drove the goat into the wilderness. In some political systems scapegoating is used as propaganda to explain national problem – blaming enemies of progress, imperialists, colonialists, and members of the opposition for policies which fail.

Schizophrenia: All conditions or illnesses, in all age groups, which are characterised from the onset by fundamental disturbances in personality, thinking, emotional life, behaviour, interests and social relationships.

The schizophrenic tends to withdraw from his/her social environment and to show a general degeneration of the personality system. The clinical traits include:

1. Withdrawal
2. Splitting:
   a Thought disorder

   b Emotional disconnections

   c Behaviour disconnections
3. Paranoid disposition
4. Abnormalities of perception

People who suffer from these symptoms are what are commonly recognized as lunatics or insane persons (Linford-Rees, 1967).

Scientia: Latin for "knowledge"; previous knowledge of operative facts; usually denotes guilty knowledge. The term is usually used in relation to fraud and refers to someone's awareness that he/she was making a false representation with intent to deceive.

Scientific method: The scientific method is a set of rules for how to establish rules required for the study and understanding of human social institutions, social issues, social problems and social facts. The scientific method enables social scientists to collect data, analyse and compare it and find possible solutions to some of the social problems, where this is possible. For effective investigation and analysis of social institutions, issues and problems, social investigators need three elements in their personal motivation, namely curiosity, scepticism and objectivity. There are seven steps to follow in scientific research:

1. Observation
2. Formulation of the problem
3. Generalisation
4. Collection and classification of facts or data
5. Formulation of hypotheses
6. Testing of hypotheses
7. Re-testing and reformulation of hypotheses
   (Hunt and Colander, 1993)

Sedition: An illegal action that tends to cause the disruption and overthrow of a government.

Seduction: Inducing an unmarried woman by means of temptation, deception, flattery or a promise of marriage to engage in sexual intercourse.

Self-defence: In law, a plea of self-defence or what is commonly termed defence of self is permissible only when the defence can show beyond any reasonable doubt that the accused acted in self-defence and that the attack on his/her own person was felonious. A felonious attack occurs when the attacker intends to kill or inflict grievous harm or to commit robbery with violence. A person is legally permitted to defend his/her person when a felonious attack is made on his/her person. He/she has a legal right to stand firm and resist, and if he kills his/her attacker during the encounter, the homicide will be justifiable, provided that the measures of resistance taken are reasonable in the circumstances. But when the attack is not felonious, then the person being attacked must, if safely possible, retreat, and must not use force against a person unless he/she is placed in such a position that he/she cannot otherwise evade the attack. He/she must flee until he/she is driven to the wall and can do nothing else.

In Selemani s/o Ussi v. Republic, the Court of Appeal for East Africa states the case as follows:

> If a person against whom a forcible and violent felony is being attempted repels force by force and in so doing kills the attacker the killing is justifiable, provided there was a reasonable

necessity for the killing or an honest belief based on reasonable grounds that it was necessary and the violence attempted by or reasonably apprehended from the attacker is really serious. It would appear that in such a case there is no duty to retreat, though no doubt questions of opportunity of avoidance or disengagement would be relevant to the question of reasonable necessity for the killing. In other cases of self-defence where no violent felony is attempted, a person is entitled to use reasonable force against an assault, and if he is reasonably in apprehension of serious injury, provided that he does all that he is able in the circumstances, by retreat or otherwise to break off the fight or avoid the assault, he may use such force, including deadly force, as is reasonable in all the circumstances. In either case if the force used is excessive but if the other elements of self-defence are present, there may be a conviction of manslaughter.

The defence of another person is lawful in so far as the person so acting uses all reasonable force to prevent the commission of a felony on another person. A criminal homicide is justifiable if the perpetrator acts without a guilty mind and believes, on reasonable grounds, that another person's life is in imminent danger and that if he had to save the other person he must act at once.

It must be noted that the defence of another person is not restricted to close relatives of the actor, such as a wife, child, parent or close friend; but that even a stranger can be defended as much as he/she can legally intervene in a fight with the hope of preventing a worse felony being committed, provided always, that he/she does so using reasonable force. Thus, a cyclist who comes down a hill and finds a person committing the felony of forcible rape, can run to the rescue of the woman and fight off the attacker, provided that he uses reasonable force. Almost the same rules apply in cases of defence of property. The criterion of legality is reasonableness. In the defence of property (even the property of others) only reasonable force is legally permitted. In all cases, the defender of property is criminally responsible for any use of excessive force.

Self-help: The right or fact or redressing or preventing wrongs by one's own action, without resorting to legal proceedings, but without breach of the peace.

Self-report studies: A modern research technique designed to measure the number of crimes committed over a period of time by asking respondents if they had committed any crime during that period. Even when the responses are suspect as regards their validity, several studies indicate that over 90 percent of the respondents admit to having committed one or two criminal acts.

Sellin, Thorsten: For several generations, Thorsten Sellin was a leading criminologist in the United States of Africa, as professor at the University of Pennsylvania in Philadelphia where, in later years, he worked very closely with Prof. Marvin E. Wolfgang. Professor Sellin's major contribution in the field of law and criminology was in the study of homicide, criminal statistics and penology, with special interest in comparative perspectives on capital punishment. His writing on capital punishment can be found in books, journals, and periodicals and in the *International Encyclopedia of Social Sciences.* Professor Sellin contributed enormously to the advancement of the study of criminology, not only in USA but also in Sweden (Wolfgang, 1968).

Senile dementia: Insanity that comes as a result of old age, progressive in character and resulting in the collapse of mental faculties in its final stage, depriving one of testamentary capacity because of the loss of power to reason or to act in a sane manner.

Sensitive personality: A sensitive person has a tendency to take offence, even when none is intended, being easily hurt and tending to brood over hurts and insults.

Sentence: Punishment ordered by a court for a person convicted of a crime. The sentence may take one of three types:

(1) sentence to death for capital offences;

(2) custodial sentence, the offender being sent to prison for a given period of time; or

(3) the sentence may be non-custodial such as a probation or a fine. Sometimes a prison term may be combined with a fine.

Sentencing: When a defendant or an accused person pleads guilty or is convicted of the offence for which he or she is accused, the court has to decide what to do with the defendant. There are three types of sentences:

1. *Determinate sentence*, in which the court has no alternative but to announce the penalty as provided by law, for example, for murder the sentence is death.

2. *Indeterminate sentence*, in which the court could sentence the convict from one day in prison to life imprisonment, or a fine of a few hundred shillings to millions of shilling.

3. *Indefinite sentence*, that is the judge finds the maximum and the minimum penalty fixed.

There are also five fine alternative penalties:

- The monetary fine
- Probation
- Corporal punishment
- Prison term
- Death penalty

Separation agreement: A separation agreed upon by the parties involved, usually drawn up by legal counsel out of court. Such an agreement may provide for sharing of property and support for the wife and the children.

Serial murder: The killing of a large number of people over time by an offender who seeks to escape detection, arrest and prosecution.

Seriatim: Latin for "in due order"; in succession; one by one.

Servant: One who works for and is subject to the control of his/

her master; a person employed to perform services for another and who, in the performance of the services, is subject to the other's control or right to control.

Settlement: Conclusive resolving of a matter, especially a compromise achieved by adverse parties in a civil suit before final judgement, whereby they argue between themselves upon respective rights and obligations, thus eliminating the necessity of judicial intervention in the dispute.

Shoplifting: Stealing from a shop or store during business hours; in law this kind of crime is not distinguished from ordinary theft.

Si vis pacem, para bellum: Latin for "if you would have peace, be ready for war".

Sine die: Latin for "without a day", means the indefinite postponement of a meeting or the proceeding of court hearing of a case.

Sine qua non: Latin for "without which not", that without which the thing cannot be; the essence of something.

Slavery: The term 'slave' was first used for white people. The word is derived from "Slav", which denotes a blond, blue-eyed people who were captured by the Germans and were reduced from being Slavs or people of glory to servitude. A slave is an individual who, involuntarily, is subjected and wholly owned and controlled by another. There are many ways in which people become slaves, the most common and most heinous being by purchase. The trading in people in Africa started in 100 AD and continued until 1440; when the Europeans joined in the trade, led by the Portuguese and later by the Spaniards, the British and the French. The first Africans to be taken as slaves were sold in an open market in the Portuguese town of Lagos, south of Lisbon. When the Portuguese extended their trade to West Africa, they established their depot in what is now Nigeria and named it Lagos; slaves were collected from Angola, Mozambique and other coastal areas and taken to

Lagos (Nigeria) before they were loaded in larger ships for the voyage to Lagos in Portugal.

A conservative estimate by UNESCO of the number of Africans that survived the journey across the Atlantic is over 210 million. This number does not include those who were shipped from East Africa to Oman before they were sent on to Arabia, India and even to China.

The slave trade was ended in 1848, not because the Europeans came to realise that the trade was evil and unChristian, but because they found it less profitable in comparison to colonialism. By then Africans had contributed to the economic development of Europe and America. In America, African slaves were encouraged to reproduce in order to provide more labour; but in Arabia, reproduction between black people was forbidden, male slaves were castrated, and as a result there are no black or mixed-race people there.

The teaching of the history of the African slave trade was never encouraged, and that explains why there is not much literature on the subject by Africans, especially in East Africa. It is only a generation or so ago that African scholars, and not politicians, began to call for reparations for colonialism and the slave trade. Europe too is beginning to stir up; the former French president Chirac declared 10 May 2006 to be a remembrance day for African slaves, slavery and the abolition of slavery, and called upon other European states that were involved in the trade to follow France's example. President Chirac called slavery an indelible stain on Europe. In 2001, the French parliament declared slavery a crime against humanity (Ajayi and Vogt, 1993; Alpers, 1967; Miers and Kopytoff, 1977; Rogers, 1961; UNESCO, 1979; Chancellor, 1987).

Smuggling: The illegal import or export of goods, especially without payment of custom duties.

Social: Of or relating to human society or its organisation; something to do with mutual relations of human beings or classes of human beings; thus there are social norms, social behaviour, social institutions, social obligations, social problems, social control, etc.

Social change: In criminology as well as in the sociology of crime and deviance, social change is regarded as a factor in the genesis of certain criminal and deviant behaviours, and abrupt social change as experienced during the process of industrialisation and modernisation offers greater opportunities for involvement in crime and deviance, especially among the youth and young adults. Social change refers to any alteration in the structure or in the function of any aspect of society. For this reason, social change is a more or less continuous and constant process characteristic of all human communities.

Social control: Social control is the most important function of criminal law. It designates those social arrangements which have been contrived in order to promote predictability of human behaviour and social regularity. Social control is contrasted with personal or individual control. Personal control is a result of socialisation, a process whereby social norms, social values and conduct are internalised to constitute a psychological mechanism that restrains behaviour and directs it to conform to socially approved behaviour. Social control is therefore external to the individual and has to be enforced by legal norms and penal sanctions.

Social control theory: This theory shows that a person's bond to his or her family and community prevents him or her from violating social rules and norms. On the other hand, when these bonds weaken, the person may engage in crime. People choose to commit crime when they lack self-control.

Social disorganisation: An area or region marked by cultural conflict; lack of social cohesiveness, transient population, insufficient social organisation, deviance and anomie.

Social function of crime: Many empirical sociologists see crime as playing a major role not only in the organisation of society but also in the way it functions; one of those was Karl Marx (1818–1883). He wrote that:

A philosopher produces ideas, a poet verses, a parson sermons, a professor textbooks, etc. A criminal produces crime; the criminal not only produces crime but also criminal law, and even the inevitable textbooks in which the professor presents his lectures as a commodity for sale in the market. There results an increase in material wealth, quite apart from the pleasure which the author himself derives from the manuscript of this textbook. Further, the criminal produces the whole apparatus of the police and criminal justice, detectives, judges, executioners, juries etc. and all the different professions, which constitute so many categories of the social division of labour, develop diverse abilities of the human spirit, and create new needs and new ways of satisfying them. Torture itself has provided occasions for the most ingenious mechanical inventions employing a host of honest workers in the production of related instruments. The criminal produces an impression, now moral, now tragic, and renders a "service" by arousing the moral and aesthetic sentiments of the public. He produces textbooks on criminal law, the criminal law itself and thus the legislatures, but also art, literature and novels. The criminal helps to interrupt the monotony and the security of bourgeois life. Thus he protects it from stagnation and brings forth that restless tension, that mobility of spirit without which the stimulus of competition would itself become blurred. He therefore gives a new impulse to productive forces. Crime takes off excess population, diminishes competition among the workers and to a certain extent stops the wages from falling below the minimum, while the war against crime absorbs another part of the same population. The criminal therefore appears as one of those natural equilibrating forces, which establish a first balance and open up a whole perspective of useful occupations.

Marx concluded with these words:

What we call evil in this world, moral or natural, is the grand principle that makes us sociable creatures, the solid basis, the life and support of all trade and employment without exception: that there we must look for the true original of all arts and sciences and the moment evil ceases, the society must be spoiled if not totally dissolved (Marx, 1964; Siegal, 1992; Mushanga, 1988).

Social problem: An alleged situation that is incompatible with the values and norms of a significant number of people who agree that action needs to be taken in order to change or alter the situation. In this respect what was a social problem a generation ago is not so to day and may not be so defined a generation to come, and what is socially acceptable today may be a social problem in future. Current social problems in Africa include poverty, ignorance, ill health, corruption, malnutrition, dictatorship and illiteracy (Earl Rubington and Martin S. Weinberg 1989, *The Study of Social Problems*, 4th edition, also D. Stanley Eitzen and Maxime Baca Zinn 1994, *Social Problems*, 6th edition).

Social science: A systematic study of organised groups of human beings. The concept of "social" refers to what pertains to human beings taken as a group as opposed to particular individuals. Social class refers to classifying people into groups or classes such as the lower class, the middle class, the upper class or the working class, and the ruling class. Science refers to a body of knowledge in respect of a particular field of natural or social phenomena. Biological science refers to the knowledge of biological things, and social science refers to knowledge of groups of people in societies. Knowledge is scientific if it has been systematically gathered, classified, explained and interpreted.

Social science is very important for modern human existence. Human beings, wherever they are in the world, are concerned with conditions of life, especially of how to preserve and prolong life, how to live together in peace and how to live happily. Knowledge of a scientific nature about life is important to all of us.

Social science, which has been divided into a number of subjects such as sociology, politics, economics, psychology, medicine, agriculture refers, in general, to all human knowledge in respect of the life of human beings. Many people feel uncomfortable when medicine or agriculture is listed as a social science subject, but for the reasons given above, whatever affects a people as a group can be considered as a topic of study under social science; and for this reason, engineering, architecture and environmental studies are social science subjects.

Knowledge of social science is becoming more and more important as societies become more and more complex in terms of their social, political, economic and legal interactions with regard to the importance of social science. Albert Einstein states: "Politics is more difficult than physics and the world is more likely to die from bad politics than from bad physics".

That is why it is very important for developing and poor countries to pay special attention to the study of social science in order to not only consolidate their national independence and reduce their dependence on their former masters, but also to eradicate internal strife, abuse of human rights and defend their people against hunger and want (Stanlislav, 1972; Elgin and Colander, 1993).

Social system: The interpersonal social relationships, social norms, values, structures and agencies within a society; a group of individuals who are in constant interaction, who are considered and consider themselves to be a social unit because of the particular culture, norms, values and objectives that bind them together.

Social work: Social work is a branch of sociology; the term is used to describe a variety of organised methods of helping people with needs they cannot satisfy unaided. In general, social workers tend to be concerned with the poor, refugees, delinquents, homeless people, the mentally ill and those who are physically disabled who, for one reason or another, need assistance and support.

Socialisation: A process that begins soon after birth, by which a person learns how to become a useful member of a particular society, learning its norms, values, customs, laws and ways of doing things. The main agents of socialisation are the family, school, peer groups, work, religion and mass media. The main methods of socialisation are direct instruction, reward and punishment, limitation, experimentation, role play, and interaction. Some agents of socialisation, such as the family and the peer group, or the family and religion, may conflict with each other by offering alternative goals, values and styles of behaviour.

Socialisation and criminality: There is an impressive amount of literature linking criminality to socialisation. Research shows that children who are raised in dysfunctional families, who experience physical and sexual abuse, whose parents are drug users, and who perform poorly in school are the ones most likely to engage in criminal behaviour. Children who maintain close bonds with the family, teachers and peer groups are the ones most unlikely to violate the law.

Society: In sociology and in related disciplines, society refers to a group of people who have lived together for long enough for them to have evolved a common culture and consider themselves to be a united and distinct social group. Society is also used to mean a group of like-minded people, such as the Uganda Bible Society, whose interest is limited to understanding the Bible message and how to spread it; or the Uganda Society for the Blind, whose main objective is taking care of and providing assistance to the blind. In this sense a society is an association.

Sociology: Derived from a Latin word *socius* meaning "companion" and a Greek word *ology* meaning "study of". The word was first employed in French by Auguste Comte (1795–1857) to mean a science of society comparable to sciences of nature in its rigour, its methods, its systematic interconnectedness and its freedom from emotion and ethical or aesthetic valuation.

Sociology of law: This is a sub-area of criminology concerned with the role social forces play in shaping criminal law and, constantly, the role of criminal law in shaping society.

Sociopath: See **psychopath.**

Solicitation: A person commits the crime if he or she solicits or incites another person to commit an offence; the solicitor is guilty of a misdemeanour whether his/her solicitation or incitement is effective or not. Thus to offer money to a medical orderly in order to be given an injection of penicillin is an offence whether the injection is given or not. Police detectives often offer money to suspects to incite them to crime, in order to arrest them red-handed, knowing that by doing so they themselves (the police detectives) are committing a crime.

Somatopsychic: The effects of a physical disease or disorders on a person's state of mind and behaviour.

Sorcery: The use of supernatural power as an aggressive instrument to further the interests of the sorcerer.

Speedy trial: A constitutional guarantee that anyone accused of a crime is entitled to a trial conducted according to prevailing rules, regulations and proceedings of the law, free from arbitrary, vexatious or oppressive delays.

Stare decisis: To stand by decided cases is a legal principle by which the decision by court in an earlier case becomes a standard with which to judge subsequent similar cases.

Static law: Shows that: "In countries of high frequency of crime against life the participation of women in these crimes is small, and vice versa; in countries of low frequency of crimes against life the participation of women in these crimes is perceptibly larger than in countries of high frequency of crimes against life" (Verkko, 1951; Mushanga, 1974b).

Status: An individual's social position, or the esteem in which he or she is held by others in society. These two forms of social prestige may be separate or interlinked. Formal social status relates to the position an individual holds as an official, for example a judge, a headmaster or a police officer. Informal social status is delivered by one's personal talents, skills or personality. Sociologists distinguish two types of status: ascribed, which is bestowed by birth; or achieved, which is a result of one's effort.

Status quo: Latin for "the conditions or positions that exist".

Statute: A statute is an act of a parliament that defines and regulates the majority of crimes and offences. The statutes, in the majority of democratic states, are passed by elected bodies of lawmakers. Thus, passing an act of parliament to regulate behaviour is a process of crime definition. The behaviour becomes criminal as soon as the parliament or any other law-making organ of a state determines so. A statute may create an entirely new crime; for instance, incest was not always a crime in Britain. A man could have sexual intercourse with an adult female whom he knew to be his sister, daughter, granddaughter or mother; but this practice was illegalised by an act of parliament when the incest law was passed in 1900. Adultery is a crime in Uganda but not in Britain, Kenya or Tanzania, because these states have never thought it fit to make such intercourse a crime, although it is allowed as sufficient cause for divorce.

Statutory declaration: A statement made under oath before a magistrate, justice of the peace, a notary public or a commissioner of oaths, giving facts relating to a person's knowledge or belief.

Statutory law: Laws created by legislative organs of the state to meet changing social conditions, public opinion and custom.

Stay: Suspension of court proceedings or the execution of a judgement.

Sub judice: Latin for "under judicial consideration"; presently before the court and therefore not subject to public debate.

Subornation: Procuring another person to commit an offence. Normally subornation is included in the offence of aiding, abetting and procuring.

Subculture: A relatively large sub-group whose social norms, and values and aspirations differ from those of the larger group of which it is part. The subculture concept is widely used in the study of deviant social behaviour or delinquency. Sociologists have shown that there are some subcultures characterised by violent behaviour such as homicide and other acts of violence (Marvin E. Wolfgang and Franco Ferracuti, 1968).

Subculture of violence: A section of a cultural group which is prone and ready to resort to the use of violence in given situations. Members of the same culture, but outside the particular subcultures, would not resort to violence in the same situation (Wolfgang and Ferracuti, 1967).

Subpoena: A command issued by the court ordering a person to appear in court at a particular place and time for the purpose of giving testimony in a specified case. The order may also require the person to present documents pertinent to the case.

Suicide: Death of an individual brought about by his or her own action; while suicide is not a crime, attempted suicide is, in many countries. A person who wilfully commits an act that may end in his or her own death is said to have committed suicide. Though successful suicide itself is not punishable, attempted suicide or unsuccessful suicide is punishable, as is assisting, aiding or advising a person to commit suicide. Emile Durkheim, one of the fathers of sociology, identified four causes of suicide. Altruistic and egoistic types of suicide result from the individual's relations with the social ideal; for altruistic, the individual is overintegrated, for egoistic, he/she is less integrated. In anomic suicide the individual is alienated from his/her social group, and is in a state of normlessness due to the weakening of his/her social ties. The fourth type is fatalistic suicide, and is due to a person's perception of the future as blocked, making life not worth living (Emile Durkheim, 1951).

Suicide, altruistic: A type of suicide common among "folk" (tribal) people who believe that by taking their own lives, they benefit others. Group welfare is highly prized. An individual will take his/her life in order to save the group from embarrassment. An elderly person may take his/her life because he/she is no longer able to make a contribution; a religious person may take his/her life because his/her conduct is unbecoming of a member of the religious group.

Suicide, anomic: Common in modern societies, where the individual feels alienated. This kind of suicide occurs when an individual experiences a downward trend in his/her life or when he/she has achieved all he/she wanted and finds nothing more worth living for.

Suicide, egoistic: Common among the industrial communities of Europe, America and Japan; suicide due to lack of social integration, individualism, financial problems, ill health, marital or occupational problems.

Suicide, fatalistic: This type of suicide results from excessive regulation in which the individual perceives his/her future as completely blocked; it was found to be common among African slaves en route to the Americas, or when faced with inhuman treatment and gross abuse.

Suicide, institutionalised: A type of suicide in which an offended person kills him/herself before the door of an offender.

Summons: A formal document issued by a court to notify a person that he or she is required to appear before court for a particular purpose at a particular place, day and time.

Superego: Part of the tripartite of the psyche; it is the ideal-oriented part of that model; an internalised consciousness that is concerned with upholding moral values of society, inculcated into children by their parents in early childhood. While the id is conceptulised as being concerned with the pleasurable aspect of life and the ego with the actual, the superego is viewed as being concerned with ideal moral behaviour.

Surety: Security in the form of money to be forfeited upon non-appearance in court, offered by the defendant or by some other person of suitable financial resources, social status or character and who, in one way or another, stands in a close relationship with the defendant. One who offers such security is also referred to as surety.

Suspended sentence: A prison sentence that does not take effect immediately. A convicted person is sentenced to a prison term, usually in the range of up to two years, and the court orders that the prison sentence be suspended for a specified term with the specific condition that its breach nullifies the suspension and the person has to go to prison. In some cases, the court may order that the person serving such a sentence be under the supervision of a probation officer.

Sutherland, Edwin H. (1883–1950): An American sociologist credited for formulating the theory of differential association or the learning theory of criminality, a process through which an individual acquires criminal or delinquent behaviour patterns. The theory states that "criminal behaviour is learnt in interaction with other persons in a process of communication" (Sutherland, 1939; Sutherland and Cressey, 1966).

T

Tax: A compulsory contribution to a state treasury by citizens and other residents conducting business within the state boundaries. There are various methods of paying tax; sometimes it is direct taxation, in some other cases it is income tax, pay as you earn, value-added tax (commonly called VAT), road tax, etc.

Tax evasion: An illegal action taken to avoid the lawful assessment of taxes, e.g. failure to declare or underdeclaring one's income.

Telephone tapping: An act of secretly listening to telephone conversations by interfering with the lines.

Tenancy: The holding or occupancy of land or buildings by a kind of right or title, especially the temporary occupancy of a house or an apartment under a lease.

Tenant: One who rents land or a building temporarily under a lease or other rental arrangement.

Tender: An offer to supply or to purchase goods or services. The offering of a tender and its acceptance normally require the parties involved to enter into a legally agreed contract. The contract sets out the details of the tender in respect of supply schedule, manner of payment, etc.

Territoriality: In international law, the term refers to the principle which provides that states should not exercise their jurisdiction outside or beyond the area of their territory. States are, however, permitted to exercise jurisdiction over their citizens in their own territory regarding illegal acts committed outside their territory. States also have jurisdiction over crimes originated within their borders but completed outside, or originated outside but completed inside their territories.

Terrorism: "Man has dominated man to his injury"(Eccl. 8:9). A recent act of terrorism was the attack and destruction of the twin towers of the World Trade Centre in New York on11 September 2001. Soon after this attack, the Pentagon, the headquarters of the Ministry of Defence of the United States of America in Washington, DC, was also attacked. The federal capital of the USA was almost destroyed in a similar manner when a plane was flown into this huge building.

Testament: A will, which deals with the testator's personal property but not his land.

Testamentary capacity: The ability to make a legally valid will. Persons who are under the legal age of majority and those suffering from some definite mental disorders are not capable of making a testament legally.

Testify: To give evidence or testimony under oath before a court or a tribunal.

Testimony: A statement made by a witness in court; usually on oath offered as evidence of the truth of what is stated.

Tête-à-tête: French meaning "head-to-head"; it means an intimate or private conversation between two people. It is common to hear that the presidents of Uganda and Kenya had a tête-à-tête at State House in Entebbe.

Thanatos: In Sigmund Freud's psychology, thanatos refers to the instinctive drive towards aggression and violence.

The bargain theory of justice: Also known as "plea bargaining" and as "copping a plea" by American prisoners. The bargaining takes place between the prosecutor for the state and defence counsel for the defendant. The bargaining seeks acceptance of the charge under which the accused pleads guilty in exchange for a reduced charge or the prosecutor's recommendation of a shorter sentence. In this legal system, a charge of murder, if accepted by the accused, is reduced to manslaughter; a charge of grand theft is reduced to petty larceny, theft of a motor vehicle is reduced to, possibly, stealing from a vehicle, rape to attempted rape, and so on. The main function of this system is not clear, except that:

1. It mitigates against severe penalties
2. It is expedient on the part of the court personne
3. A plea of guilty satisfies the prosecution by relieving it of the burden of court and office work; for without the willingness of suspects to accept the charges, the police and courts would find it impossible to handle the bulk of the cases before them
4. The defence counsel is satisfied, as is the offender, for securing a lesser charge and hence lesser penalty. The practice of plea bargain is widely used in the USA. A study carried out in 1956 of felons convicted in one district court showed that 93.8 percent had entered a plea of guilty; recidivists were found to be more ready to plead guilty than non-recidivists

In some cases offenders benefit from the plea bargain, especially if the prosecution is likely to open several cases, as is common in criminal cases such as:

a) being armed in public
b) resisting arrest
c) possession of firearms without a permit
d) being in possession of a loaded firearm, etc.

Under this system all these charges are ignored and only one is recorded and then the penalty is usually lenient or probation.

The holy three of criminology: The three great Italian scholars commonly referred to as the "holy three of criminology" are:

1. Cesare Lombroso (1835–1909), a medical doctor who specialised in mental disorders, later became interested in finding out which physical traits characterise criminals and published *L'Uomo Delinquente* in 1876 *(The Criminal Man)*, in which he showed that criminals can be identified by physical features, and are atavistic in nature.
2. Enrico Ferri (1856–1929), referred to by Thorsten Sellin, as "one of the most colourful and influential figures in the

history of criminology". He was an extremist sociologist lawyer, a member of parliament, a journalist and a professor.

3. Raffael Garofalo (1852–1934) was an anthropologist and professor of law.

The three holy men of criminology agreed that more emphasis should be given to the criminal person him/herself and his/her treatment, rather than to the criminal act and penal sanctions or punishments (Schafer, 1976).

Elements of an offence: A person is not criminally responsible for an act unless it is proved that he/she actually committed the act voluntarily and with malice.

The law requires that it be proved that:

a He/she did contribute directly or indirectly
towards the commission of a criminal offence or what is commonly called *actus reus* and in so doing, acted.

b Of his/her free will, that is voluntarily, and

c With a guilty mind, or *mens rea*.

The concepts of *actus reus* and *mens rea* have their origins in a statement by Sir Edward Coke, attorney general of England at the beginning of the seventeenth century, when he stated: *Actus non facit reum nisi mens sit rea* (an act does not make a man guilty unless his mind is blameworthy) (Smith and Hogan, 1972).

Theft: Dishonest appropriation of property belonging to someone else with the intention of keeping it permanently. Theft by use of force may amount to robbery.

Third party insurance: Insurance against risks to persons other than those that are parties to the policy. It is illegal to use or to allow anyone else to use a motor vehicle on a road unless there is a valid insurance policy covering death, physical injury, or damage by the use of the vehicle. Anyone driving a motor vehicle is obliged to give his/her name and address and that of the car owner and to produce the certificate of insurance when ordered to do so by a traffic police officer at once or at a police station within a given time.

Threat: The expression of an intention to harm someone with the object of forcing him/her to do something against his/her will. Threat is a common element in many criminal acts such as criminal damage, duress, forcible entry, intimidation, racial hatred, rape etc.

Tort: Derived from old Latin which meant "twisted" or "wrung" and now means any civil wrong committed against an individual. Generally speaking, a tort is a violation of one's private rights not grave enough to be considered a crime. A tort is committed against an individual if his/her person, property or character is harmed by a wilful or negligent act of another. For this reason, any nuisance that amounts to the violation of an individual's rights is a tort. For example, playing loud music after midnight while other people want to sleep is a tort, as is allowing one's dog to bark and disturb the neighbours (Readers Digest Association, 1975).

Torture: The convention against torture and other cruel, inhuman and degrading treatment or punishment was signed on 10 December 1984. Torture is defined as: -

> Any act by which severe pain or suffering, whether physical or mental is intentionally inflicted on a person for such purposes as obtaining from him or a third person information or a confession, punishing him for an act he or a third person has committed or is suspected of having committed or intimidating or coercing him or a third person, or for any reason based on discrimination of any kind, when such pain or suffering is inflicted by or at the instigation of or with the consent or the acquiescence of a public official or other person acting in an official capacity. It does not include pain or suffering arising only from, inherent in or incidental to lawful sanctions (Shaw, 1997).

Trafficking: In respect of narcotics, manifesting, selling, giving, administering, transporting, sending, delivering or distributing, or offering to do any of the above.

Transferred intent: If an illegal yet intended act results from intent to commit a crime, that act is also considered to be illegal.

Transnational crimes: Criminal acts committed across transnational borders; these include smuggling, illicit import or export of goods without permit, drug trafficking, transportation of human beings for sale as slaves or sexual workers etc.

Transparency: In a democratic state, transparency is a requirement to ensure that reasons behind measures and the applicable regulations are clear to all, so that all are treated fairly. Transparency International is a world-wide organisation based in Berlin, Germany, that carries out surveys on corruption around the world and lists nations according to the extent of corruption. For some years African nations such as Nigeria, Kenya and Uganda have appeared among the most corrupt.

Transportation: A penal sanction in which a convicted person is sent away from home, formerly a common practice in Britain where offenders were transported to colonial territories, especially Australia. Portugal used to transport murderers, rapists, misfits and all manner of delinquents and vagabonds to Angola and Mozambique.

Transsexual: A person who believes and feels that he or she belongs to the sex opposite to his or her gender at birth. It is now possible for those who believe they belong to the opposite sex to undergo surgical operations to alter their sex, i.e. a man may have all his male sex organs removed and replaced with an artificial vagina. In addition to the operation, hormonal drugs are administered to promote the desired sexual orientation and features.

Treason: Betrayal of loyalty to the state as in an act of attempting to overthrow a legally constituted government.

Treaty: An international agreement in writing between two states (bilateral treaty) or a number of states (a multilateral treaty). Such treaties are also known as conventions, pacts, protocols, final acts or arrangements.

Trespass: A wrongful interference with another person or with his/her possession of land or goods. Such acts as striking a person, entering his/her house or land or taking his/her goods are trespass cases.

Trial: A trial is the hearing of a civil or criminal case before a court of competent jurisdiction. Trials must be heard in public except when the court decides that the hearing must be conducted in camera.

Trial within a trial: The preliminary examination by a judge of a witness to determine his/her competence or to determine the admissibility of an item of evidence such as a confession.

Tribe: A human group speaking a distinctive language or dialect and possessing a distinctive culture that distunguishes it from other groups; it need not be politically organised or confined to a single nationality. For example, some groups of people on the Kenya-Uganda border are separated from each other by an international boundary, with some groups being in Kenya while others are in Uganda.

Trust: An entity or organisation that holds assets for the benefit of certain other persons or entities.

Trustee: One who holds legal title to property in trust for the benefit of another person, and one who is required to carry out specific duties with regard to the property, or one who has been given power affecting the disposition of property for another person.

Tu quoque: Latin for "you too"; used to denote a type of argument that descends to the level of simply saying "you too", that is, accusing the accuser of having the same fault as his/ her accused. A common example of this word is "physician heal thyself".

Turpitude: Usually used as in moral turpitude, meaning behaviour that is contrary to justice, honesty and morality.

U

Ultra vires: Beyond strength, beyond powers. The term is used in law to denote any action which is beyond the legal powers of a particular body to take. An official organ of the state or committee can be said to have acted ultra vires if it exceeded its powers or limits.

Unconscious: Of thoughts, experiences, and feelings, going on without our awareness. According to Freud, this lack of awareness is a result of repression.

Unconstitutional: Something is said to be unconstitutional if it conflicts with some provision of the constitution. If it is a statute, it is considered to be void or as if it had never existed.

Undue influence: The improper use of any power or threat so that consent is not voluntary.

Unlawful assembly: The meeting of three or more people with the intent to disturb the peace; if the disturbance becomes tumultuous the assembly becomes a riot.

Unnatural act: Any of the several types of sexually deviant behaviour such as homosexuality, sodomy or bestiality. These acts are considered crimes in most Third World countries, but in industrialised countries, they are no longer considered as deviant behaviour but are termed orientations and are therefore not considered to be criminal.

Unnatural offences: These are crimes against nature; they include acts such as sodomy, buggery, bestiality etc.

Usurpation: An unlawful seizure or occupation of another's property, privilege or power.

Usury: Originally it meant charging of any interest on money; now it refers to charging an exorbitant rate of interest.

Utmost resistance: The degree of resistance that a woman is required to offer her attacker in order to charge him with rape or attempted rape.

V

Vagina dentata: Latin for "vagina with teeth". In the sphere of mental states it symbolises fear of castration, fear of sexual intercourse, fear of returning to the womb and fear of rebirth.

Vagrancy: Not having any visible means of support; not having a fixed home or employment; vagabondage.

Vagrant: One who is idle and disorderly; also one who is a peddler and one who trades without a licence; a prostitute who behaves indecently in a public place; also one who begs in public places.

Valid: An act or a decision that has legal strength and force, is binding, sufficient and effective to be held by the courts.

Vandalism: Any act of defacing or damaging property for no apparent reason. In many jurisdictions vandalism is covered under criminal damage.

Variance: The discrepancy between statements or legal documents; any divergent or inconsistent factor.

Verbum sapienti sat est: Latin for "a word to the wise is enough".

Verbals: Any remarks an accused person makes in the presence of the police and recorded by the police, which may be read out as evidence at the trial.

Verdict: A jury's finding on matters referred to it in a criminal or civil trial. The usual practice is that the jury reaches its verdict in secret and no subsequent inquiry can be made as to how it was reached.

Verification: Confirmation of correctness or authenticity of pleading or other paper affidavit, oath or disposition; an affidavit attached to a statement insuring the truth of that statement.

Versus: Latin for "towards" or "against", used in law and sports.

Veritas odium parit: Latin for "truth begets hatred".

Vest: To confer legal ownership of land or rights on someone.

Vested interest: A complete right, not depending on any future event.

Veto: In international law, a veto is the power enjoyed by a member state to block a unanimous decision; it simply refers to a refusal to agree with the rest of the members, thereby making a majority decision null and void. At the United Nations Security Council, five member states have vetoes; these are France, China, Russia, United Kingdom and the United States of America.

Vicarious liability: The liability of a person through the act of another; as where the master is liable for the negligence of his/her servant.

Vice: Indulgence in wicked or immoral conduct; moral fault.

Vicinage: Refers to a neighbourhood, vicinity or a particular area where a crime was committed; where a trial is being held.

Victim: A victim of crime is any person or a group of persons who suffers damage, loss or injury as a result of criminal conduct perpetuated by another person or group of persons (Mushanga, 2004).

Victim–precipitated crime: A criminal act in which the victim was responsible for its occurrence; for example, in many homicide cases, the victim is found to be the first to strike the offender; or to produce a deadly weapon such as a gun, spear or knife with which he or she is killed.

Victimless crimes: These are crimes that are common but have no victims or complainants, including sexual misconduct such as prostitution, sodomy, homosexuality, buggery and such offences as the use of marijuana, and being idle and disorderly.

Victimology: A study of the victims of crime focusing on the nature of crime, the circumstances under which crime is committed, the personal characteristics of the victim and the offender; and the relationship between the offender and his/her victim. For example, violent crimes such as homicide, battery and grievous assault are commonly committed between people who know each other or who are related; even crimes like rape are often committed by offenders who know the victim.

Victimology also includes the study of the role of the victim in bringing about his or her own victimisation. For example, the failure by the victim to take the orders of the offender seriously, for example when the offender tells the victim. "I will shoot you if you do not get away," the victim may enrage his or her adversary by answering, "Shoot me, who are you anyway?"

Violence: The use of physical force by an individual or by a group against another individual or a group of people or property with the intention of causing harm, injury or destruction. For example, it is an act of violence to attack a person with a knife and stab him/her in the back.

Violence may breed violence: It has been established that children who witness or are subjected to violence in their earlier years very often develop violent attitudes later in life. The following is an example of this:

> In 1985 in Wyoming, U.S.A. a 16 year-old youth shot and killed his father. The boy testified that very often his father beat him and cursed him; and that his father very often made excuses to go into the bathroom whenever his 15-year old sister was having a shower, and that he had actually seen his father fondling his sister. He also said that his father often beat his mother, which was corroborated by the mother. On the day of the incident, there was a terrible family argument, after which the father and mother went out for supper; on their return, the daughter and

186

son had decided to kill the father, and they did. The son was sentenced and served three years, and his sister's prison term was commutted; she was released after serving one week (Reid 1987).

Violent crime: Any act which involves the use of force or the threat of the use of force against the person of another. Any act which is done with the intention of causing fatal consequences for or injury against the person of another (Mushanga, 1976).

Violent disorder: An offence when three or more persons present together use or threaten unlawful violence. Violence includes violent conduct towards property as well as persons and extends to conduct causing or intended to cause injury or damage.

Voir dire: A process in which a potential jury panel is questioned by the prosecution and defence lawyers in order to select objective and unbiased persons to serve as jurors.

Virtue: The observance of accepted moral standards; personal excellence; chastity especially in a woman.

Vis-à-vis: French derived from Latin *visus,* meaning sight or "appearance" but now means face-to-face, as having a face to face meeting with another person.

Vis major: Latin meaning "a greater force" in civil law; denotes an act of God; an irresistible natural course that cannot be guarded against by ordinary exertion of skills and prudence.

Vitiate: To void; to render a nullity; to impair.

Viz: (videlicet) Latin, meaning "namely".

Vox populi: Latin for "voice of the people", Latin maxim *vox populi, vox Dei,* i.e. the voice of the people is the voice of God, which means that the will of the mass of the people must prevail, a common political slogan.

Voyeurism: Obtaining sexual pleasure from spying upon a stranger while he or she is naked or is engaged in a sexual activity.

W

Waiver: The giving up or relinquishing of one's rights such as the right to counsel or to a jury trial.

Wolfgang, Marvin E. American criminologist, educated at Dickinson College, and at the University of Pennysalvania for his MA and PhD and where he taught for almost all his life. He authored many books, the most important being *Patterns in Criminal Homicide* (1964), *Studies in Homicide* (1967) and *Crime and Culture, Essays in Honour of Thorsten Sellin* (1968).

Professor Wolfgang was president of the American Society of Criminology and a member of a number of commissions on national criminal law reform of the USA.

Wanton: Grossly negligent or careless; with a careless disregard for consequences.

War: Legally, war is a state of affairs that exists when two or more states resort to the use of force to vindicate rights or to settle disputes between them. In international law, a state of war exists when a party to the dispute declares its decision to go to war or when hostilities flare up between belligerent parties.

Ward: A person whom the law regards as incapable of managing his/her own affairs, and over whom or over whose property a guardian is appointed.

Warrant: A writ issued by a court authorising a law enforcement officer such as a police officer to arrest or search a suspect or place.

Weapon: An instrument for offence or defence. In crimes of violence, common weapons used to inflict harm or death include firearms, spears, knives, pangas, axes and any sharp instrument.

Weapons of mass destruction: A recent concept that has been popularised by the American leadership after the attacks of 11 September 2001. Weapons of mass destruction refer to nuclear weapons, including atomic bombs and other highly sophisticated destructive equipment. Countries which possess these weapons include China, France, the United Kingdom, the United States, Russia, India, Israel and North Korea. A dread of weapons of mass destruction weighed so heavily on the psyche of the American president George W. Bush, that he launched an attack on Iraq erroneously, believing that the country, under the leadership of Saddam Hussein, was in possession of weapons of mass destruction.

White–collar crime: Crimes committed by persons of respectability and high social status in the course of their occupations. These crimes are widespread but are not frequently reported to the police. Persecution is frequently avoided because of the political or financial impotence of those concerned, or because of the difficulty in securing evidence sufficient for prosecution. (Sutherland and Cressey 1974; Sutherland, 1949).

White-collar crime and social harm: Excepting violent crime, white-collar crime has been found to cause more social harm than common street crime such as burglary, mugging, robbery, and petty theft. The theft of money meant for a maternity clinic causes more harm to society than several bank robberies.

Why do people commit crime? Historically speaking, criminologists, as a group, have focused on identifying why individuals commit crime. The earliest criminologists placed great emphasis on genetics, medical or even biological explanations. Later, they focused on psychiatric, psychological and psycholanalytic explanations; this in turn was replaced or superseded by the sociological explanations, which are currently dominant. Explanations for why people commit crime are sought in their social backgrounds and the circumstances of their upbringing rather than in individual shortcomings of a psychological nature. As everyone knows, there is no single cause of crime, crime is caused by a multiplicity of factors, and these relate to social milieu, economic status, family structure and functions, sex and age, education, and the legal and criminal law system. The sociological explanation is that crime is learnt in a social setting. More specifically, a person becomes a criminal because of an excess of definitions favourable to the violation of a law; people, therefore, become criminals because of their contact with criminal patternand because of their isolation from anti-criminal pattern (Sutherland and Cressey, 1966).

Will: This is a person's declaration of how he or she desires his/her property to be disposed of after his or her death. When a person dies without a will, he/she is said to have died intestate.

Wilful: Intentional, not accidental; in criminal law, it signifies an act done with a bad purpose and without justifiable excuse.

Witchcraft: It is the use of magic or sorcery for the advancement of personal interests; very widely practised in Africa, especially by illiterate and semiliterate persons, although there are indications that even educated people engage in this practice. It is a symptom of intellectual backwardness and lack of enlightenment.

Witness: One who gives evidence in a case before a court and who attests or swears to facts or gives testimony under oath.

Work release: An arrangement by which a prisoner is given permission to leave prison for the purpose of attending an educational institution, to work at a job in the community and return to prison every evening. Work release is also known by others as work parole, outmate programme, day work, daylight parole and intermittent imprisonment.

Writ: A legal order issued by an authority and in the name of the state to compel a person to do something therein mentioned. In every case the writ contains directions for doing what is required.

Writ of certiorari: Latin meaning "to bring the record of a case from a lower court up to a higher court for immediate review".

Writ of prohibition: A prerogative writ issued by a superior court that prevents an inferior court or tribunal from exceeding its jurisdiction or usurping jurisdiction it has not been given by law.

Wrongful act: Any act that in the ordinary course will impinge upon the rights of another to his/her damage.

Y

Youthful offenders: Young persons who are accused of crime and processed through juvenile rather than adult courts; they are treated as juvenile delinquents rather than adult criminals and when found guilty, they should ideally be sent to a juvenile facility and not to an adult prison.

Z

Zealous witness: A witness who displays undue favouritism towards one party in the case.

Zero tolerance: Denotes a political commitment by political leaders to eradicate corruption or any other pressing social problem.

Zombie: Someone who lacks energy and seems to act without thinking and is not aware of what is taking place around him or her.

Bibliography & References

Adeyemi, Adedokum A., "Corruption in Africa: A Case Study of Nigeria", in Tibamanya Nwene Mushanga (ed.), 2004 *Criminology in Africa*, Fountain Publishers, Kampala

Adler, Mortmer J., 1991, *The Great Books of the Western World*, Encyclopedia Britannica, London

Ajayi, Ade J.A. and M.O. Vogt (eds.), 1993, *Proceedings of the First Pan African Conference on Reparations*, 27-29 April, Abuja, Nigeria

Alpers, E.A., 1967, *East African Slave Trade,* East African Publishing House, Nairobi

Amnesty International, 1978, *Report on the Conference on Death Penalty,* AJ Index CDP 02/02/78 9 August 1978, Amnesty International, Stockholm

Amos, William E., Raymond L. Maneka and Manlyn L. Southwell, 1965, *Action Programmes for Delinquency Prevention*, Thomas, Springfield, Illinois, USA

Andeneas, Johannes, 1974, *Punishment and Deterrence*, Ann Arbor, Michigan

Andreski, Stanslav, 1972, *Social Science as Sorcery*, Andre Deutsch, London

Angeles, Peter A., 1992, *The Dictionary of Philosophy*, 2nd edition, Harper Collins

Asuni, Tolani, "Drug Trafficking and Drug Abuse in Africa" in Tibamanya Mwene Mushanga (ed.), 2004, *Criminology in Africa*, Fountain Publishers, Kampala

Awake 2001, *The New Look of Terrorism*, 22 May 2001

Barnes, Harry Elmer, 1930, *The Story of Punishment: A Record of Man's Inhumanity to Man*, Stafford Co., Boston

Bedau, Hugo Adam, 1964, *The Death Penalty in America, An Anthology*, Aldine Publishers, Chicago

Bedau Hugo Adam, 1970 *The Death Penalty as Deterrence: Argument and Evidence*, Ethics 80, NBO. 3

Bohannan, Paul (ed.), 1960, *African Homicide and Suicide*, Princeton,1964 New Jessey

Bottomore, T.B., 1964, *Karl Marx: Selected Writings in Sociology and Philosophy*, McGraw Hill, New York

Brown, Dan, 2003, *The Da Vinci Code*, Anchor Books, New York

Buss, A.B., 1961, *The Psychology of Aggression*, John Wiley, New York

Chalk, F. and K. Jonassohn, 1989, *The History and Sociology of Genocide*, Yale University Press, New Haven, Connecticut, USA.

Chancellor, William, 1987, *The Destruction of African Civilization*, Third World Press, Chicago, USA

Clinard, Marshall B. and Robert F. Meier, 1998, *Sociology of Deviant Behavior*, 10th edition, Harcourt Brace & Co., New York

Clinard, Marshall B. (ed.), 1964, *Anomie and Deviant Behabviour. A Discussion and Critique*, Free Press, New York

Ayo, John, 1999, *Dictionary of Foreign Words in English*, Wordsworth Editions Ltd.

Clinard, Marshall B. and Daniel J. Abbott, 1973 *Crime in Developing Countries: A Comparative Perspective*, John Wiley, New York

Clinard, Marshall B. and Peter C. Yeager, 2006 *Corporate Crime, Transaction*, New York

Clinard, Marshall B. and Richard Quinney, 1973, *Criminal Behavior Systems: A Typology*, 2nd edition, Holt, Rinehart and Winston

Davis, G.R.C., 1971, *Magna Carta*, British Museum, London

Davis, Kingley, 1949, *Human Society*, Macmillan, New York

Dicey A.V., 1885, *Law of the Constitution*, London

Dicey A.V., 1884, *Introduction to the Study of the Constitution*, London

Durkheim, Emile, 1951, *Suicide*, translated by John A. Spraulding and George Simpson, Free Press, New York

Eitzen, D. Stanley and Maxim Daca Zinn, 1994, *Social Problems*, 6th edition, Allyn and Bacon Publishers

Ekirikubinza, Lillian Tibatemwa, 1995, *More Sinned Against than Sinning*, Copenhagen

Everret, Suzanne, 1978, *History of Slavery*, Bison Books Ltd, London

Gardner, Gerald, 1956, *Capital Punishment as a Deterrent and its Alternative*, Victor Gollancz

Gifis, Steven S., 1993, *Dictionary of Legal Terms*, 2nd edition, Barions

Gleitman, Henry, 1981, *Psychology*, 2nd edition Norton, New York

Gourevich, Philip, 1998, *We Wish to Inform You That Tomorrow We Will be Killed with Your Families*, Farrar, Straus and Giroux, New York

Hartjen, Clayton A., 1974, *Crime and Criminalization*, Praeger Publishers, New York

Haskell, Martin R., and Lewis Yablonsky, 1974, *Criminology, Crime and Criminality*, Rand, M., 1990 (ed.), *Political Corruption*, Holt, Rinehart and Winston, New York

Hochschild, Adam, 1998, *King Leopold's Ghost*, Macmillan, London

Hoebel, F. Adamson, 1966, *Anthropology: The Study of Man*, McGraw Hill Company, New York

Humana, Charles, 1992, *World Human Report Guide*, OUP, London

Hunt, Elgin F. and Donald C. Colander, 1997, *Social Science: An Introduction to the Study of Society*, 8th edition, Macmillan, London

Huntington, Samuel P., 1970, "Modernization and Corruption", in Anold J. Heidenheimer, 1970 (ed.) *Political Corruption*, Holt, Rinehart and Winston, New York

Kabba, Muctaru, "Ritual Homicide in Sierra Leone", in Tibamanya Mwene Mushanga (ed.), 2006, *Criminology in Africa*, Fountain Publishers, Kampala

Lacey, A.R., 1993, *A Dictionary of Philosophy*, 3rd edition

Lambo, T. Adeoye, 1962 "Malignant Anxiety: A Syndrome Associated with Criminal Conduct in Africans", in *Journal of Mental Science*

Lindner, Robert, 1961, "Homosexuality and Contemporary Society", in *Must You Conform?* Grove Press, New York

Linford-Rees, W.L., 1967, *A Short Textbook of Psychiatry*, English University Press, London

Lipset, Seymour Martin, 1963, *The Political Man: The Social Basis of Politics*, Anchor Books, New York

Lloyd, Dennis, 1970, *The Idea of Law*, Cox and Wymann Ltd, London

Macllan, David, 1980, *The Thought of Karl Marx*, 2nd edition, Macmillan

Mannheim, Herman, 1939, *The Dilemma of Penal Reform*

Mannheim, Herman, 1941, *War and Crime*

Mannheim, Herman, 1965, *Comparative Criminology*, Vol. 1 & 11, Boston

Marshall, Gordon, 1998 (ed.), *Dictionary of Sociology*, Oxford University Press, New York

Martin, Elizabeth A., 1997, *Dictionary of Law*, Oxford

Marx, Karl and Fredrick Engels, 1848, *The Communist Manifesto*, London

Middendorff, Wolf, 1971, *Punishment For and Against*, Hart, New York

Miers, Suzanne and Igor Kopytoff (eds.), 1977, *Slavery in Africa*, University of Wisconsin Press, USA

Mitchell, Duncan, 1968, *A Dictionary of Sociology*, Routledge and Kegan Paul, London

Moser, Joy, 1979, *Prevention of Alcohol-Related Problems*, WHO, Geneva

Mushanga, Tibamanya Mwene, 1974, *Criminal Homicide in Uganda*, East African Literature Bureau

Mushanga, Tibamanya Mwene, 1974, *Crime and Deviance: An Introduction to Criminology*, East African Literature Bureau

Mushanga, Tibamanya Mwene, 1977, *Homicide and its Social Causes* (unpublished)

Mushanga, Tibamanya Mwene (ed.), 2004, *Criminology in Africa*, first published by UN Institute for Prevention of Crime in Rome 1992, and later by Fountain Publishers, Kampala

Mushanga, Mwene, 2006 *From Generation to Generation* (unpublished)

Mushanga, Tibamanya Mwene, 2000, *Social Causes of Homicide* (unpublished)

Mushanga, Tibamanya Mwene, 1994, *Genocide and Suicide in Rwanda and Burundi: A Response to Centuries of Racial Inequality* (unpublished).

Mushanga, Tibamanya Mwene, 1995, *Slavery and Colonial Exploitation of Africa: A Case for Reparation* (unpublished)

New Africa magazine, October 1999, London

Newman, Donald J. and Patrick R. Anderson, 1989, *Introduction to Criminal Justice*, 4th edition, Random House, New York

O'Connor, Anthony, 1991, *Poverty in Africa*, Belhaven Press, London

Odera, Henry Oruka, 1976, *Punishment and Terrorism in Africa*, East African Literature Bureau

Oxford Dictionary of Quotations, 1980

p'Bitek, Okot, 1973, *Africa's Cultural Revolution*, Macmillan, Nairobi

Pan, Lynn, 1975, *Alcoholism in Colonial Africa*, The Finnish Foundation for Alcoholic Studies, Vol. 22, Helsinki

Pervin, Lawrence A., 1984, *Personality*, John Wiley, New York

Popkin, Richard H., and Avrum Stroll, 1993, *Philosophy Made Simple*, 2nd edition, London

Puzo, Mario, 1998, *The Godfather*, Arrow Books, London

Readers Digest, 1975, "You and the Law" Canada Readers Digest Association, Montreal, Canada.

Radzinowicz, Sir Leon, 1966, *Ideology and Crime*

Redmond, P.W.D. and Shears, Peter, 1997, *General Principles of English Law*, 3rd edition, Pitman Publishing, London

Reid, Sue Titus, 1987, *Criminal Justice*, West Publishing Company, New York

Roger, J.A., 1961, *Africa's Gift to America*, New York

Rousseau, Jean J., 1762, *Social Contract*

Rubington, Earl and Martin S. Weinberg, 1989, *The Study of Social Problems*, OUP, London

Saleemi, N.A. and Ateenyi, T.K., 1998, *Elements of Law*, N.A. Saleemi Publishers, Nairobi

Scarpitti, Frank R. and Paul T. McFarlane, 1975, *Deviance: Action, Reaction and Interaction*, Addison Wesley Publishing Company, Reading, Massachusetts, USA

Schafer, Stephen, 1976 *Introduction to Criminology*, Reston Publishing Company, USA

Schur, Edwin, 1965, *Crimes Without Victims*, Prentice Hall, New Jersey

Sellin, Thorsten, 1967, *Capital Punishment*, Harper and Row, New York

Sellin, Thorsten, 1937, "The Lombrosian Myth in Criminology", in *The American Journal of Sociology*, 24 May

Sellin, Thorsten, 1938, *Culture, Conflict and Crime*, Social Science Research Council, New York

Sellin, Thorsten, 1958, "Recidivism and Maturation", *National Probation and Parole Association Journal*, July

Shaw, M.N., 1997, *International Law*, 4th edition, Cambridge University Press

Shur, Edwin M., 1965, *Crimes Without Victims*, Prentice Hall, New Jersey.

Siegel, Larry J., 1992, *Criminology*, 4th edition, West Publishing Co., New York

Smith, David and Collin Simpson, 1970, *Mugabe, Pioneer Head*, Salisbury, Zimbabwe

Smith, J.C., and B. Hogan, 1972, *Criminal Law*, 2nd edition, Butterworth, London

Stanslav, Andreski, 1972, *Social Science as Sorcery*, Andre Deutsch, London

Sutherland, Edwin H., 1949, *White Collar Crime*, Holt, Rinehart and Winston, New York

Sutherland, Edwin H. and Donald R. Cressey, 1974, *Criminology*, 9th edition, J.B. Lipponcott, New York

Sutherland, Edwin H., and Donald R. Cressey, 1973, *The Principles of Criminology*, 9th edition, J.B. Lippincott, New York

Sutherland, Edwin H. (ed.), 1937, *The Professional Thief by a Professional Thief*, University of Chicago Press, Chicago

Sutherland, Edwin H., 1939, *Criminology*

The Penal Code of Tanzania

The Penal Code of Uganda

The World Almanac and Book of Facts, 2005 World Almanac Books, New York

Toennis, Ferdinand, 1955, *Community and Association*, East Lansing University Press, Michigan

Tylor, Edward B., 1871, *Primitive Culture*, New York

UNESCO, 1979, *The African Slave Trade*, East African Publishing House, Nairobi

Van Bemnele, J.B., 1968, "New Ways of Punishment" in Marvin E.Wolfgang (ed.) *Culture and Crime: Essays in Honour of Thorsten Sellin*, John Wiley and Sons, New York

Verkko, Veli, 1951, *Homicide and Suicide in Finland*, Copenhagen

Vold, George, B., 1970, *Theoretical Criminology*, OUP, London

Wolfgang, Marvin E., 1958, *Patterns in Criminal Homicide*, Philadelphia, at University of Pensylvannia.

Wolfgang, Marvin E. and Franco Ferraculti, 1968, *The Subculture of Violence*, Tavistock, London

Wolfgang, Marvin E., Leonard Savitz and Norman Johnston (ed.), 1970, *The Sociology of Crime and Delinquency*, 2nd edition, John Wiley and Sons, New York

Wolfgang, Marvin E., 1966, *Patterns in Criminal Homicide*, John Wiley

Wolfgang, Marvin E. (ed.), 1968, *Culture and Crime: Essays in Honour of Thorsten Sellin*, John Wiles, New York

Wolfgang, Marvin E., and Franco Ferracuti, 1967, *The Subculture of Violence*, Tavistock, London

World Almanac, 2005

Zimring, Franklin E. and Gordon J. Hawkins, 1973, *Deterrence*, University of Chicago Press

Index

204

LaVergne, TN USA
20 August 2009
155414LV00002B/207/P